Beginner's
POLISH

Beginner's
POLISH

Wanasz-Białasiewicz
OF
EUROLINGUA

HIPPOCRENE BOOKS
New York

To my children

Luiza and Seweryn

For information, address:
HIPPOCRENE BOOKS, INC.
171 Madison Avenue
New York, NY 10016

ISBN 0-7818-0299-7

Printed in the United States of America.

TABLE OF CONTENTS

INTRODUCTION

The rich culture and language of Central and Eastern Europe are unique, intricate and subtle, steeped in tradition by hundreds of years of history. Yet, since the Eastern European countries remained essentially closed societies for over 40 years under communist rule, little is known about them.

With the fall of the Iron Curtain, a flurry of activity is being spurred throughout Eastern Europe by the desire to establish democratic institutions and free market economies. Firms from the West are exploring business opportunities and expansion into these virtually untapped markets. A fresh and beautiful land together with the rich and exciting cultural heritage of its people has opened up for tourists to explore.

EUROLINGUA was started in September 1990 to meet the growing demand for Central and Eastern European languages and cross-cultural instruction. Our goal is to primarily serve tourists and business people who deal in international trade.

Insight into the people and customs of a country is vital to the enjoyment of a trip for most consummate travelers. Similarly, successful international transactions necessitate knowledge of local rules of conduct in various business situations. But most importantly, basic information about the geography, history and politics of the country to be visited, along with rudimentary language knowledge will make anyone feel more at home.

It is the above considerations that have brought about this book, in the hope that it will become your friend and guide during your trip. The knowledge of customs, manners and some basics of language should help you enjoy your visit to the fullest, while helping you make friends and contacts among the locals.

The book has two parts. The first gives you information about the country (geography, history, economy, culture, customs and manners), while the second part consists of language lessons.

The language lessons are designed for a traveler or a non-specialist amateur. You will learn useful phrases and words for special situations as well as basic grammar hints. The lessons will not cover all grammatical problems, nor will they give a rich vocabulary for sophisticated conversation. Instead they will teach you enough to feel comfortable in a variety of situations, which you will find described here.

We hope that with this small, compact book you will have in your pocket a collection of bits of information, sufficient to carry out satisfying conversations with the people of the country you visit, in their own language. It is the result of many hours of work, research and travel done by enthusiastic teachers and travelers who wish you good luck in your study and a wonderful trip.

GEOGRAPHY

Poland is a country located in Central Europe. Its surface area is 312,683 sq. km (120,727 sq. miles) and it has a population of 38 million inhabitants. Administratively, Poland is divided into forty-nine voivodeships (provinces). Its border is 3,538 km (2,198 miles) long, including 524 km (326 miles) of seacoast.

Poland is a lowland country; its average height above sea level is 173 m (562 ft.). A characteristic feature of Poland's land structure is the parallel arrangement of geographic regions. Going from south to north, one may distinguish: mountain chains (the Sudetes and Carpathians); the Silesian, Little Poland, and Lublin highlands; the Central Polish lowland; the Pomeranian and Mazurian lake regions; and the Baltic coastal strip. The country's highest point is Mount Rysy in the Tatra Mountains, 2499 m (8119 ft.). The longest rivers in Poland are the Wisła (Vistula) which is 1047 km (651 miles) long and the Odra (Oder) of which 742 km (461 miles) flow through Poland. These rivers traverse Poland from south to north. Poland's largest lakes, the Śniardwy and Mamry, are located in the Mazurian Lake Region.

The capital of The Republic of Poland (Rzeczpospolita Polska) Warszawa (Warsaw), is a city of over 1,5 million inhabitants located on the Vistula river. The country's 38 million inhabitants are largely of Polish nationality. 2/3 of the population lives in 830 towns and cities. Poland is a young country: 30 per cent of its inhabitants have not reached working age. 90 percent of Poles declare themselves as Catholics.

Major cities: Warszawa (1,532,000 inhabitants), Łódź (818,000), Kraków (713,000), Wrocław (593,000), Poznań (534,000), Gdańsk (444,000), Szczecin (381,000) and Katowice (350,000).

Climate. Poland lies in a temperate climate zone; its weather is halfway between oceanic and continental. A distinctive feature of Poland's climate is the presence of six seasons. A generally freezing winter lasts from the middle of December to the end of February. A changeable and capricious pre-spring sometimes continues even through the first half of April when it usually gives way to a warm spring during which frosts may occur as late as May. A warm and sunny summer lasts from June through August. The "Golden Polish

Autumn" occurs during the sunny and dry months of September and October. November is the month of the pre-winter, which precedes the snowy winter. The average annual temperatures range between 5 and 8.5 degrees Celsius, depending on the part of the country. In the summer temperatures can exceed 30 degrees Celsius in the shade, while in winter they rarely fall below -20 degrees Celsius.

HISTORY AND POLITICS

The landmark in the process that led to the creation of the Polish state was the adoption of Christianity in 966 by Prince Mieszko I. Mieszko united the Slavonic tribes which inhabited the area roughly corresponding to Poland's present territory. His son, Bolesław Chrobry, consolidated the new state and became its first king, crowned in 1025. His successors made up the Piast dynasty, which ruled till the 14th century, at first from Gniezno, and later from Kraków. After its demise, the Polish throne went to the Lithuanian Jagiellonian dynasty. Poland and Lithuania were joined by a personal union, superseded by a real union in the 16th century. After their victory over the Teutonic Order, the Jagiellonians began to expand their state eastwards and become the most powerful ruling family in continental Europe: their dominions included Poland, Lithuania, Bohemia and Hungary, and extended from the Baltic to the Black Sea.

After the death of the last member of the dynasty Poland become an elective monarchy. Kings were elected by the gentry and the throne went to Polish aristocrats or members of European royal families. The 17th century was a period of wars which sapped the country's strength in spite of a number of great victories. Attempts at reforming the state, undertaken by the last king in the second half of the 18th century, were brought to an end by the partitions of Poland between Austria, Prussia and Russia. After the final partition, Poland's king Stanisław August Poniatowski abdicated and Poland ceased to exist as an independent state.

Poles did not give up hope of regaining independence. They raised a large army which fought alongside Napoleon, took part in the Spring of Nations of 1848 and twice rebelled against Russian domination, meeting defeat in both cases. The independent Republic of Poland was finally reborn (for a brief period of 21 years) in 1918 after the defeat of the partitioning powers. Its borders, the result of wars with Germans, Ukrainians and Soviet Russia, were confirmed by the Treaties of Versailles and Riga.

In 1939 Poland stood up to Hitler and was defeated after a short struggle and Soviet invasion from the East. In spite of a double occupation, Poles created the structures of an underground state and a resistance movement. A government in exile resided in London and Polish soldiers fought on almost all fronts of the war. 6 million citizens of Poland lost their lives between 1939 and 1945.

The Yalta accords signed by the allied powers imposed new frontiers on Poland coupled with Soviet domination and the communist system. Poles, however, did not accept the new, totalitarian order. A series of protests culminated in 1980 with a nation-wide wave of strikes which opened the way for creation of the independent trade union "Solidarity". Even the imposition of martial law in December 1981 was not able to stop the process of change and arrest the decay of the communist system. After elections held as a result of the round table talks in 1989 the opposition entered Parliament, and in September 1989 the first non-communist government was formed.

ECONOMICS

Thus far Poland can be characterized as a country of missed economic opportunities. The political changes of the last years, however, mean that Poland's natural advantages have become more attractive to investors. Poland is located between Western Europe and the countries formerly belonging to the Soviet Union, and its reasonably good transport network enhances this geographical advantage. It has considerable natural resources (coal, electrolytic copper production) and a labor force which for many years will remain cheaper than in the developed economies of the West. The political changes in Poland are accompanied by rapid moves towards a market economy. Many Poles have shown an entrepreneurial spirit, which was suppressed under communism. A banking infrastructure is being built, businessmen are forming business societies, investors are being offered favorable conditions, the currency has become convertible. The Polish government has embarked on a wide ranging program of restructuring and privatizing of state industrries. Changes in agriculture will be helped by the fact that private ownership of land was preserved in Poland, sole among Eastern Block countries. The Polish economy is finally opening up to the world.

Major industries. Poland is one of the largest producers of numerous industrial goods in the world. The country is number four in Europe in the production of mining machinery and equipment. Sulfur and pyrite resources have become the basis for the development of the production of sulfuric acid and equipment with which it is made. Copper, which has only recently been discovered in Poland, has been largely responsible for a production increase in the electrical engineering industry. Some of Poland's most successful exports are rolling stock cars and electrical locomotives. The achievements of the post-war shipping industry are also worth looking at. The shipyards in Gdańsk, Gdynia and Szczecin produce sea-going vessels for the most demanding customers. Polish yachting craft have successfully sailed round the world and triumphed in Atlantic races.

Natural Resources. Nature has generously endowed Poland with all the basic necessary resources for a modern economy. Mineral coal resources (70,000 million tons up to a depth of 1,000 m), brown coal, and gas have enabled Poland to take second place in Europe in the production of energy raw materials in spite of an almost complete lack of petroleum. The abundance of rich deposits of cooper, lead and zinc, sulfur, rock salt, potassium and the wealth of raw materials for construction purposes (limestone, marl, gypsum, granite, and sandstone) have enabled Poland not only to satisfy her own needs for the development of Polish industry but have also permitted her to export considerable quantities of raw materials. Materials imported in large quantities include petroleum, iron ore and phosphorites.

ARTS

The traditions of Polish culture and scholarship go back to the Middle Ages. The Jagiellonian University in Kraków, founded in 1364, is among the five oldest academic establishments in Europe. Its graduates include the great astronomer Nicolaus Copernicus.

Major monuments of the past include the Wawel Royal Castle in Kraków or the Renaissance town of Zamość in the east of the country. But it is the spiritual heritage that is primarily responsible for the historical continuity and universal relevance of Polish culture.

The composer Frederic Chopin was born in Poland; he began composing while still in Poland and Polish folk music motifs permeate his work. Chopin piano competitions are organized in Warsaw every five years, attracting talented young musicians from all over the world. Polish contemporary music flourishes as well, with composers such as Krzysztof Penderecki, Andrzej Panufnik, Witold Lutoslawski and Henryk Górecki. Poland also has a vibrant jazz community (jazz became immensely popular in the 1950's just after the end of the Stalinist period). Leading Polish jazz musicians include Michał Urbaniak or the late Krzysztof Komeda, who has scored a number of Roman Polański's films.

Polish film is currently in an evolving period, which may still come to match the great days of Polish cinema in the late 50's. "The Decalogue", a series of films by Krzysztof Kieślowski, won the European Cesar Award, Andrzej Wajda's 'Man of Iron', a film about the 1970 and 1980 workers' strikes in Gdańsk won the Golden Palm at the Cannes Film Festival in 1981, while at the 1990 Cannes Film Festival the Polish actress Krystyna Janda was awarded a prize for her main role in Ryszard Bugajski's 'Interrogation'.

Polish experimental theater has also won a permanent place on the stages of the world thanks to the work of Tadeusz Kantor and Jerzy Grotowski. Sławomir Mrożek is the best know contemporary Polish playwright.Three Polish writers were awarded the Nobel prize for literature: the novelist Henryk Sienkiewicz, the author of 'Quo Vadis?', Władysław Reymont (both in the first quarter of this century) and most recently, the poet Czesław Miłosz (1981).

Today, Poland is a country at a European crossroads, where a variety of cultures and cultural spheres converge.

PRACTICAL ADVICE FOR EVERYDAY LIFE

A foreigner who is not well acquainted with Polish customs may be taken by surprise by norms and ways of behavior that differ from those found in Western Europe and the US.

TRANSPORT AND COMMUNICATIONS

Roads

The best way of traveling to Poland is by plane or car. The roads are good. There are four basic classes of roads in Poland
- motorways
- main roads - all international highways designated with the letter "E" and highways linking Poland's chief towns.
- secondary roads - local roads linking other localities.
- other roads.
All roads in Poland, irrespective of their class, are provided with a full range of road signs. So are the transit routes across the cities. Along the main roads, drivers and tourists can repose on car park sites located in the most scenic spots. The more frequented roads are dotted with roadside motels, many of which offer good meals and a sound night's sleep in cozy rooms.

The speed limit for automobiles:
     - in heavily populated areas - 60 km p.h.
     - elsewhere - 90 km p.h.
The speed limit for caravan-trailers-autos:
     - in heavily populated areas - 60 km p.h.
     - elsewhere - 70 km p.h.
In towns and heavily populated areas the public transportation vehicles pulling of the stop have the right of way.

Road Service

In the event of car trouble on the road, the driver can get help by calling the nearest road service center. Such help is given both by state firms and private shops.A specialist in services of this kind is the Office of Automobile and Motorcycle Federation (BTM PZMot), which offers help to the following persons:

- members of automobile clubs that belong to the Federation Internationale de l'Automobile-FIA or Alliance Internationale de Turisme-AIT
- holders of 'Mondial Assistance' or 'Europ Assistance" insurance.

BTM PZMot offers or consigns the following services in this regard:
- repair of damaged cars in service stations,
- hauling or repatriation of damaged cars,
- medical assistance, including hospital care,
- import of spare parts required for repairs.

Fuel

The filling station network is sufficiently dense. Lead-free fuel, however, can be bought only in larger towns. Color codes for fuel types are:

red	98	octane gasoline (premium)
yellow	94	octane gasoline
green	86	octane gasoline

The letters ON stand for diesel fuel.
The price per one liter of gasoline is at the average European rate.

Public Transportation

Buses and Tramways - these are the cheapest means of transportation in every city. Before boarding, buy a ticket at a nearby 'RUCH' news stand, then cancel it in a special machine once on board.

Taxi

Because of inflation, the charge on taxi meters is multiplied by a factor that should be clearly displayed in the vehicle. Alternatively, the driver and passenger should agree on the price beforehand. In Warsaw, call radio taxi at telephone 919.

Car Rentals

It is recommended to arrange the rental before departure through your travel agent. In Poland, you can make necessary arrangements in ORBIS RENT A CAR at the airport or near the Forum Hotel or BUDGET or HERTZ at the airport or the Marriot Hotel in Warsaw. Other cities where you can rent a car are: Kraków, Gdańsk, Wrocław, Katowice, Łódź, Szczecin. International driver's license is required.

Touring by Train

Railroads connect Poland with many cities in Europe. The extensive network of Polish Railways (PKP) provide good connections even with the smallest towns throughout Poland. Most trains carry two classes: first class for more comfortable travel and second for economy. The swiftest connections are by fast inter-city trains or by express trains.

Communications

Postage stamps are sold at post offices. International phone calls can be made from post offices (operator calls, direct dial) or from hotel/private home phones (direct dial). Tokens for telephone booths can be bought at post offices and hotels. Post offices in towns are open in the hours 8-20, (8 A.M.-8 P.M.) but are closed on Saturdays and Sundays. In large cities, one post office remains open 24 hours a day.

Using tokens can prove to be a problem with long distance calls. Magnetic cards are much easier to use. Telephones accepting magnetic cards have been installed in the majority of Warsaw hotels. They can also be found at Okęcie Airport, at the railway stations and main post offices. Soon they will be also available on the streets of major cities. There are two kinds of cards. One has a capacity of 50 units. The other contains 100 units.

Use AT&T Calling Card to call the US and more than 65 countries. AT&T operator: 0-010-480-0111.

Important phone numbers in Warsaw

Police: 997
Fire Brigade: 998
Ambulance: 999
Operator (international) 901
Operator (domestic) 900
Sending telegrams: 905
Car towing service: 987, 954
Agency for Foreign Investment in Poland: 285061
Ministry of Foreign Affairs: 287451
Ministry of Foreign Economic Relations: 6935000
Fax machines are available at post offices.

MONEY

The Polish monetary unit is 1 złoty (abbr. zł) which consists of 100 groszy (abbr. gr.). Three bank notes are in circulation, with values 10, 20, and 50 zł. A large range of coins exists. These are the following: 1, 2, 5, 10, 20, and 50 gr as well as 1, 2, and 5 zł. Foreign currency is best exchanged in banks or bureaux de change (Polish name 'kantor'). The current exchange rate is displayed there. Foreign visitors are advised to avoid unofficial currency trades. Credit cards are not very common in Poland and can be used only in some hotels, shops and restaurants. Traveler's checks are accepted in banks. Banks usually open at 8 AM and close at 1 PM except Saturdays and Sundays.

SHOPPING

Shops are generally open from 11 AM to 7 PM. Department stores open earlier and close later (without a lunch break). 24-hour shops are rare. Products of Polish folk arts and crafts are available in CEPELIA shops; DESA offers fine art, painting, sculpture; PEWEX stores have a wide selection of imported goods of all kinds.

Clothing Sizes

Women's Dresses, Etc.

British	32	34	36	38	40	42	44
American	10	12	14	16	18	20	22
Continental	30	32	34	36	38	40	42

Men's Suits

British and American	36	38	40	42	44	46
Continental	46	48	50	52	54	56

Men's Shirts

British and American	14	$14^1/_2$	15	$15^1/_2$	16	$16^1/_2$	17
Continental	36	37	38	39	41	42	43

ELECTRICITY

Voltage is 220 AC, 50 cycles. American plugs do not fit Polish outlets. Bringing along your own adapters and transformers is advisable.

RESTAURANTS

The art of cooking has a long tradition in Poland. Some typical dishes are: beetroot soup, sour soup, hunter's stew, pork chop with cabbage, ravioli with cheese, and beef tripe.
In Poland the gastronomic system consists of:

Restaurants which are divided into several categories from luxury to category IV. As a rule they serve a full range of meals, i.e. breakfast, dinner and supper. Besides separate restaurants located in all cities, higher category hotels also operate such facilities. In many cities there are specialized restaurants which serve Polish regional and foreign dishes. Higher category restaurants also provide entertainment.

Bars also serve full range of meals, but are intended for quick, volume business. With prices lower than in restaurants, the most popular are the milk bars, which serve vegetarian dishes made on milk and milk by-products bases as well as vegetables.

Coffee-shops serve: coffee, tea, cold beverages, pastries, alcohol (wines, brandies). Coffee-shops in hotels also serve breakfast. In Poland coffee-shops are typical places for social rendezvous.

Cocktail-bars serve: milk cocktails, ice cream, beverages, pastries.

Inns serve a full range of meals like restaurants.

In Poland breakfast is served from 7-10 AM., dinner 1-5 PM., and supper 6 - 9 PM.

The proper way to use your utensils is a little different from the American way. Eat with your knife in the right hand and the fork in your left hand throughout the meal.

RECREATION AND TOURISM

Poland is a country of many young people and recreation activities play an important role in everyday life.

All large cities have stadiums where a variety of sporting events take place, but these structures are also available for public use such as jogging or riding your bicycle.

There are a large number of parks which are ideal for quiet walks and relaxation. All cities have public swimming pools, as do most large hotels. Tennis courts belong primarily to athletic clubs.

It is not advisable to ride your bicycle in large cities due to heavy traffic. In some areas specially designated bike paths are in use. They are marked with an international pictograph showing a white bicycle on blue background.

A number of private health clubs as well as golf courses are also beginning to spring up around the country.

Weekend trips outside of the city are very popular, as most Polish metropolitan areas lie within easy reach of forests, rivers or lakes.

The Polish mountain regions with the town of Zakopane, known as the 'winter capital of Poland', at the foot of the Tatry mountains (highest peak: Rysy 2499 m), offers spectacular views along with ample opportunities for skiing, hiking and rock climbing. The Mazury lakes are choice spots for kayaking, canoeing, waterskiing or simply relaxing and catching some fish. The Baltic coastline (500 kilometers) with wide sandy beaches is also a popular vacation destination.

Unique and valuable parts of the country make up National Parks and nature reserves. Each has its special attraction. The Puszcza Białowieska forest is a unique ecosystem where the last European Bison roam free, among a great variety of other wild game. In the Pieniny national park raft trips are organized down the Dunajec river where it cuts through the Pieniny mountains in a picturesque gorge. The Ojców national park offers the unusual sight of medieval and renaissance castles perched high on limestone cliffs.

The solitary walker will find peace, tranquillity and unspoiled nature in the Bieszczady mountains in the southeast. Finally, dense woods throughout the country offer many opportunities for camping or hunting. Hunters will find wild boar, deer, hare and pheasant. Hikers can freely walk through forests and across meadows, even when they are private property.

Poland's towns and cities contain valuable architectural monuments. The Old Town of Kraków and Warszawa have been listed as Class '0' monuments by UNESCO (sites designated as constituting part of mankind's cultural heritage). A further class '0' monument is the Salt Mine in Wieliczka (near Kraków) with underground chambers and statues carved in rock salt. Many smaller towns offer a unique experience as well, such as Zamość, Kazimierz Dolny, Książ or Opatów. In northern Poland many interesting monuments can be found in towns which in the 13-14th centuries belonged to the Teutonic Knights: the magnificent castle in Malbork, or fortified cathedral in Frombork. Other interesting monuments of the past include the municipal fortification in Paczków, and the park and palace complexes ranging from Kórnik (near Poznań) in the west, through Wilanów in Warsaw, to Łańcut in the southeast.

Connoisseurs of modern art can visit a museum of socialist-realist art established in the palace in Kozłówka near Lublin, the final home of monuments of communist heroes which until recently stood in the market squares of many Polish towns.

INTRODUCTION / FAREWELLS

Greetings in Poland are more **formal** and more guided by rules than in America. Formal greetings are:

> dzień dobry - good morning
> do widzenia - good -bye
> dobry wieczór - good evening
> dobranoc - good night

While shaking hands is the common form of greeting, men often kiss ladies' hands. It is customary to introduce a lady to a gentleman and a subordinate to a superior, as well as a younger person to an older person. The same applies when a handshake is called for.

You may greet a younger person or someone you know very well in an **informal** way:

cześć - Hi
serwus- Hello

VISITING

Poles are a hospitable nation, and like to spend their time in good company. Guests invited home (one can be late by 15 min. to half an hour) will be entertained generously.

It is not polite to come empty handed. If you happen to be invited to a party at a Polish home, don't forget to give your host a bunch of flowers. The Poles are crazy about flowers! They love to receive them and they do receive them on every occasion, even the least important. Candy or a bottle of wine also make good gifts.

Strong alcoholic drinks are usually drunk undiluted.

CLEANERS

Pralnia is a generic name of the company which offers dry cleaning and laundry services. Express or normal service is available.

HOLIDAYS

The following public holidays are observed:

New Year's Day	1 January
Easter Monday	date varies
Labor Day	1 May
3rd May Constitution	3 May
Corpus Christi	date varies
Assumption	15 August
All Saints Day	1 November
Polish National Day	11 November
Christmas	25 and 26 December

All offices, schools and shops are closed on these days.

TIME / CALENDAR

Poland is in the Central European time zone. Time differences compared to Warszawa include:

New York: - 6 hours   London: - 1 hour   Los Angeles: - 9 hours

Poland uses daylight savings time from the end of March until the end of September.

Days of the week

poniedziałek	- Monday
wtorek	- Tuesday
środa	- Wednesday
czwartek	- Thursday
piątek	- Friday
sobota	- Saturday
niedziela	- Sunday

Seasons

wiosna	spring
lato	summer
jesień	fall
zima	winter

Months of the year

styczeń	- January
luty	- February
marzec	- March
kwiecień	- April
maj	- May
czerwiec	- June
lipiec	- July
sierpień	- August
wrzesień	- September
październik	- October
listopad	- November
grudzień	- December

Asking for time:

time	czas
hour	godzina
minute	minuta
second	sekunda

What is the time?	Która godzina?
It's eight o'clock.	Jest ósma.
It's quarter to eight.	Za kwadrans ósma.
It's half past eight.	Wpół do dziewiątej.
It's ten minutes past eight.	Dziesięć po ósmej.
At what time?	O której godzinie?
In two hours.	Za dwie godziny.
Between nine and ten.	Między dziewiątą a dziesiątą.
When?	Kiedy?
In ten minutes.	Za dziesięć minut.
How long will it take?	Jak długo to potrwa?

Time of the day

morning	rano
before noon	przed południem
at noon	w południe
in the afternoon	po południu
evening	wieczór
in the evening	wieczorem
night	noc
at night	w nocy
day	dzień
during the day	w ciągu dnia

THE POLISH LANGUAGE

The Polish language belongs to the group of Slavic languages, which constitute the Indo-European family of languages along with the Germanic, Romance and several other linguistic groups.

The Slavic languages developed from one common predecessor, the Proto-Slavic language. Initially divided into three dialects, the East, West and South Slavic, Proto-Slavic gave rise to the various Slavic languages. The most widespread among them at present is Russian, which belongs to the Eastern group. Among the west Slavic languages, Polish is the largest. It is spoken by 38 million people in Poland and by some five million abroad. Polish has a recorded tradition of 850 years and very rich literature which flourished particularly during the literary periods of the Renaissance (the 16th century) and Romanticism (the 19th century). The post-war years have seen a new era in Polish literature. During these years the social and political changes in Poland resulted in a considerable democratization of literary (or standard) Polish and in the wide distribution of literary works among society.

Polish has some characteristic phonetic features, e.g. nasal vowels and three parallel series of dental, alveolar, and palatal consonants. Another important feature is the tonic stress, which is always placed on the penultimate syllable of the word.

As with the majority of Slavic languages, Polish is inflected, i.e. nouns, pronouns, numerals and adjectives are differentiated according to case and numbers (declension), while verbs change their forms according to persons and tenses (conjugation).

LANGUAGE LESSONS

PRONUNCIATION GUIDE

Here are some general tips concerning Polish pronunciation:

Most Polish polysyllabic words stress the last syllable but one

      domy - houses   **ro**wer   - bicycle
      do**bra**noc - good night   infor**ma**cja - information

Monosyllabic words unite with the preceding or following word

      na **sto**le - on the table   na ro**we**rze - on bicycle

In some verbial forms and words of foreign origin ending with -ika, -yka, -ik, -yk, the stress falls on the third syllable (counted from the end)

      byłyśmy - we were   **mu**zyka - music
      mate**ma**tyka - mathematics

Polish spelling is fundamentally phonetic i.e. one letter of the alphabet corresponds to one sound. Some sounds are marked by combinations of two letters: cz, dz, dż, dź, sz, rz, ch. Others are marked with diacritical marks: ą, ć, ę, ń, ó, ś, ż, ź, ł.

THE POLISH ALPHABET

Latin characters are employed in Polish as in English, but as the pronunciation differs in the two languages, we give below all the Polish letters and combinations of letters, with their sound in alphabetical order.

VOWELS: a, e, i, o, u, (ó), y, ą, ę

CONSONANTS: b, c, d, f, g, h, (ch), j, k, l, m, n, p, r,   s, t, w, z
                      ch dz   ń   rz ś   ź
                      ć dź   s   ż (rz)
                      cz dż

Letter	Pronunciation	Examples
a	like **u** in English cut	Janek - Johnny
ą	like French **on** nasal vowel	mąż - husband
b	like **b** in English book	baba - old woman
c	like **ts** in English its	cukier - sugar
ć	like **ch** in English cheap	ćwiczyć - practice
ci	before vowels as **c**	ciocia - aunt
ch	like **h** in English half	chleb - bread
cz	like **ch** in English church	czas - time
d	like **d** in English daughter	daleko - far
dz	like **ds** in English woods	chodzę - I go
dź	like **j** in English journey very softly pronounced	łódź - boat
dzi	before vowels as **dz**	dziadek - grandfather
dż	like **j** in English judge	gwiżdżę - I whistle
e	like **e** in English best	teraz - now
ę	like **in** in French fin nasal version of **e**	męża - of the man
f	like **f** in English from	farba - paint
g	like **g** in English go	góra - mountain
h	like **h** in English house	hotel - hotel
i	like **ee** in English bee	wino - wine
j	like **y** in English you	Jan - John
k	like **k** in English token	kawa - coffee
l	like **l** in English leaf	lalka - doll
ł	like **w** in English wet	łamać - to break
m	like **m** in English man	matka - mother
n	like **n** in English name	noc - night
ń	like soft **n** in English new	koń - horse
ni	before vowels onion	niania - nan
o	like **o** in English Tom	nowy - new
ó	like **u** in English put	córka - daughter
p	like **p** in English palace	pokój - room
r	like **r** in English three	gra - play
rz	identical in sound with z like **s** in English pleasure after p, t, ch, it is as **sh** like in English shine	rzeka - river trzy - three
s	like **s** in English soft	salon - sitting room
ś	like **sh** in English she	iść - to go

sz	like **sh** in English shop	**sz**afa - cupboard
t	like **t** in English table	**t**alerz - plate
u	like **u** in English food	d**u**ży - big
w	like **v** in English vest	**w**oda - water
y	like **i** in English milk	s**y**n - son
z	like **z** in English zeal	**z**abawka - toy
ź	like **s** in English measure	we**ź**mie - he will take
ż	like **s** in English pleasure	**ż**aba - frog

LEKCJA PIERWSZA

ZAPOZNANIE

Dwie pary spotykają się w samolocie do Warszawy:
Jan i Ewa Kowalscy, Maria i Józef Urbaniak.

Jan: Czy mogę się przedstawić? Nazywam się Jan
Kowalski a to moja żona Ewa Kowalska.

Józef: Przyjemnie mi państwa poznać. Nazywam się Józef
Urbaniak a to jest moja żona Maria Urbaniak. Przepraszam,
ale słyszę lekki akcent w pana angielskim?

Jan: My jesteśmy Polacy. Opuściliśmy kraj ponad 10 lat temu
i mieszkamy w USA. Będziemy się dziwnie czuć po tak
długiej niebecności.

Maria: Zobaczycie państwo duże zmiany! Czy macie rodzinę
w Polsce?

Ewa: O tak, dużą.

Józef: Zapewne nie mogą się doczekać, aby was zobaczyć.

Jan: Tak się składa, że nie będziemy mieli dużo wolnego czasu;
to jest głównie podróż służbowa.

Józef: Czym się państwo zajmujecie?

Jan: Ja jestem adwokatem a moja żona ekonomistą. Prowadzimy
Międzynarodową Firmę Konsultingową i myślimy
o założeniu oddziału w Warszawie.

Józef: Życzę sukcesów. Ja pracuję w handlu zagranicznym
i wiem, że jest duże zapotrzebowanie na tego rodzaju firmę.

Jan: Może będziemy mogli współpracować w przyszłości!

LESSON ONE

INTRODUCTIONS

Two couples meet on a plane on the way to Warsaw.
Jan and Ewa Kowalski, Maria and Józef Urbaniak.

Jan: Please allow me to introduce myself. My name is Jan Kowalski and this is my wife Ewa Kowalski.

Józef: Nice to meet you. My name is Józef Urbaniak and this is my wife Maria Urbaniak. Do I detect a slight accent in your English?

Jan: We're Polish but we left the country over 10 years ago and have been living in the USA since. It's going to be odd to be coming back after such a long time.

Maria: You will see a lot of changes! Do you still have family in Poland?

Ewa: Oh, yes, quite a large one!

Józef: I'm sure they can't wait to see you.

Jan: Unfortunately we won't have much free time; this is primarily a business trip

Józef: Oh, what do you do for a living?

Jan: I'm a lawyer and my wife is an economist. We run an International Consulting Firm and we're thinking of establishing a branch office in Warsaw.

Józef: It will be a success! I work in foreign trade myself and I know that there is a large demand for such businesses!

Jan: Maybe we could work together some day!

VOCABULARY

adwokat	lawyer
akcent	accent
ale	but
będzie (być)	it's going to be (to be)
czasie (czas)	time
dwie	two
do	to
długi	long
doczekać (czekać)	wait
dużo	much
dziwnie	odd
głównie	primarily
handel	trade
i	and
interes, firma	business
jest	is
ja	I
ja jestem	I am
kraj	country
lat, lata	years
lekki	slight, light
mieli (mieć)	have (to have)
mi	to me, for me
moje	my
mieszkać	live
my	we
nie	no
nazywam się	my name is
opuścić	left
oddział	branch
międzynarodowy	international
noc	night
pary	couples
podróż	trip
proszę	please
przyjemnie	nice
przepraszam	sorry
przedstawić	introduce
prowadzić	run
poznać	meet

razem	together
rodzina	family
samolot	plane (airplane)
twoim (twój)	yours
pracować	work
wolny	free
w przyszłości	some day
was	you
wyczuwać	detect
zapewne	for sure
zapoznanie	meeting
zmiany	changes
żona	wife

ZWROTY

EXPRESSIONS

Czym sie pan zajmuje?	What do you do?
dużo zmian	a lot of changes
Nazywam się . . .	My name is . . .
Miło mi pana/panią poznać	Nice to meet you
Pozwolą państwo, że się przedstawię	Please allow me to introduce myself
dzień dobry!	good morning!
dobry wieczór!	good afternoon!
do widzenia!	good-bye!
dobranoc!	good night!
dziękuję!	thank you!

OBJAŚNIENIA

EXPLANATORY NOTES

dzień dobry!

may be used in the meaning of 'good morning', 'good afternoon', sometimes even in the meaning of 'good evening' .

proszę

here you are; here it means **please** and is used at the begining of a sentence.

Jak się pan/pani miewa?

How are you? How do you feel?

EXERCISES

1. Copy the text, read it aloud and translate it.

2. Drill the phrases:
   Dziękuję. Proszę. Dzień dobry!

3. Translate into Polish:
   Good morning. Good evening. Thank you. How are you?
   Good-bye.

4. Translate into English:
   Dzień dobry pani. Dzień dobry! Jak się pani ma? Doskonale.
   A pan? Dziękuje, dobrze. Do widzenia!

ZAPAMIĘTAJ	REMEMBER
Ewa, Maria	feminine names
Jan, Józef	masculine names
nie czekać	the negation *nie* is put **before** the verb

GRAMMAR

WORD ORDER

The word order in a Polish sentence is much more elastic than in English; though the natural word order is also:

SUBJECT - VERB - OBJECT etc.

Adverbials and particles may be put either at the beginning or the end of the sentence, or even in the middle, e.g.:

tego chłopca nie znam - that boy I don't know (literal translation)

nigdy nie byłem w Warszawie - never I was not in Warsaw

często widzę ją na ulicy - often I see her in the street

NEGATIVE AND INTERROGATIVE SENTENCES

To form negative sentences **nie** (not) is placed **before** the verb in Polish, even if there is another negative word in the sentence, e.g., **nigdy nie** byłem. (I never was). In English only one negative is permissible in a sentence, but the Poles say: 'I never was not'.

Interrogative sentences are formed by placing the interrogative particle **czy** at the beginning of the sentence, not by reversing the positions of the subject and the verb, as in English, e.g.: Czy pan X jest w domu? (Is Mr.X at home?).

THE FAMILIAR AND POLITE FORM OF ADDRESS

In the so-called 'familiar' form of address, the personal pronouns **ty** (you-Sg.) and **wy** (you-Pl.) are used with the second person Singular and Plural, respectively, of the verb. This form is employed when addressing relatives, intimate friends and children.

The 'polite' form of address consists of the word **pan** (Mr., Sir, gentleman) for male persons and **pani** (Mrs., madam, lady) for female persons, and is conjugated with the third person of the verb, e.g.: Czy ma **pan** bilet? (Have you a ticket?). This form is used when addressing individuals, acquaintances, strangers and superiors; **państwo** when addressing couples (Mr. and Mrs.) or groups of people.

EXERCISE

1. Write the following sentences in the Interrogative Form.

   Example: Pan Urbaniak czeka na panią Kowalską.
   Czy pan Urbaniak czeka na panią Kowalską?

   a. Jan czeka na Ewę.
   b. Józef zna pana B.
   c. Pan A. przeprasza pana B.

LEKCJA DRUGA

PRZYLOT / WYNAJĘCIE SAMOCHODU

Pasażerowie wysiadają na lotnisku Warszawa-Okęcie.

Józef: Oto nasz telefon i adres. Proszę, zadzwońcie w tym tygodniu.

Jan: Było nam bardzo przyjemnie państwa poznać i na pewno będziemy w kontakcie.

KONTROLA PASZPORTOWA

Kontroler: Proszę paszport.

Jan: Proszę

Kontroler: Dziękuję. Czy mówi pan po polsku? Pana nazwisko jest Kowalski.

Ewa: Tak, opuściliśmy kraj 10 lat temu.

Kontroler: Rozumiem. Jak długo zamierzają państwo pozostać?

Jan: Dwa tygodnie.

Kontroler: Czy będą państwo mieszkać u rodziny?

Jan: Nie, w Hotelu Victoria.

Kontroler: Dziękuję. Proszę przejść do kontroli celnej.

KONTROLA CELNA

Celnik: Dobry wieczór. Czy macie państwo coś do oclenia?

Jan: Nie, tylko rzeczy osobiste i małe prezenty dla rodziny.

Celnik: Czy może pan otworzyć dużą walizkę?

Jan: Proszę bardzo.

35

Celnik: Wszystko w porządku. Proszę przejść.

WYPOŻYCZALNIA SAMOCHODÓW

Jan: Patrz, tam jest biuro Hertza. Możemy wynająć samochód.

Hertz Rep: Dobry wieczór. Czym mogę służyć?

Jan: Chcemy wynająć samochód na 2 tygodnie.

Hertz Rep: Czy wybrali państwo konkretny model?

Jan: Mały samochód wystarczy.

Hertz Rep: Mamy Volkswagen Golf za $500 na tydzień.

Jan: Czy w cenę jest wliczony przebieg?

Hertz Rep: Tak, łącznie z ubezpieczeniem.

Jan: Bardzo dobrze, bierzemy.

LESSON TWO

ARRIVAL AT AIRPORT / RENTING A CAR

The passengers have disembarked at Warszawa-Okęcie Airport.

Józef:　Well, you've got our telephone number and address. Give us a call sometime this week.

Jan:　We're very glad to have met you and we will definitely stay in touch.

PASSPORT CONTROL

Officer:　Passport please.

Jan:　Here you go.

Officer:　Thank you. Do you speak any Polish?　Your last name is Kowalski.

Ewa:　Yes, we left the country 10 years ago.

Officer:　I see. How long do you plan on staying?

Jan:　Two weeks.

Officer:　Are you going to be staying with your family?

Jan:　No, at the Hotel Victoria.

Officer:　Thank you. Please proceed to customs.

CUSTOMS

Officer:　Good evening. Do you have anything to declare?

Jan:　No, just personal belongings and same small presents for our family.

Officer:　Could you please open the large suitcase?

Jan:　There you go.

Officer: Everything is in order. Please proceed.

CAR RENTAL

Jan: Look, there's the Hertz office. We can rent a car.

Hertz Rep: Good evening, how may I help you?

Jan: We'd like to rent a car for two weeks.

Hertz Rep: Do you have any preference?

Jan: A small one will do.

Hertz Rep: We've got a Volkswagen Golf for $500 a week.

Jan: Is that with unlimited mileage?

Hertz Rep: Yes, and it includes insurance too.

Jan: Perfect. We'll take it.

VOCABULARY

adres	address
aha	I see
bardzo dobre	perfect, very good
benzyna	gasoline
bierzemy	we take
celnik	duty officer
chcielibyśmy (chcemy)	we would like
cło	duty
czy	do you, if
czy będziecie ...	are you going to ...
czy macie	do you have
czy to jest	is that
długo (długi)	long
dobry	good
dziękuję	thank you
gdzie	where
gotowe	ready
hotel	hotel
ile	how much
jak	how
tak	yes
kiedy	when
kontrola	control
kontroler	officer
kontrola celna	custom
lotnisko	airport
łącznie	includes
macie (mieć,mamy)	you have, to have,we have
mam	I have
małe	small
mieszkać	stay, live
móc (możemy)	can, we can
nazwisko	last name
naprawić	repair
na pewno	definitely, surely
nasz	our
nieograniczony	unlimited
nie podlega ocleniu	duty free
nowe	new
numer	number

mogę (móc)	may, can
mówić	speak
opona	tire
opuściliśmy	left
osobiste	personal
otworzyć	open
planować	plan
pani	Mrs. , You
pan	Mr. , You
państwo	Mr. and Mrs, You
pasażerowie	passengers
paszport	passport
patrz	look
po polsku	in Polish
prezenty	presents
przebieg	mileage
przebita opona	flat tire
pomoc	help
poznać, znać	meet, know
porządek (w porządku)	order, in order
przechodzić	proceed
przyjemnie	glad, nice
rozumiem	I see, understand
rzeczy	belongings
samochód	car
stacja benzynowa	gasoline station, pump
tam	there
tak	yes
telefon	telephone
tutaj	here
tydzień (tygodnie Pl.)	week, weeks
tylko	just, only
w kontakcie	in touch
zapotrzebowanie	demand
założyć	establish

ZWROTY

EXPRESSIONS

Czy macie zamiar . . .?	Are you going to...(do something)?
W czym mogę pomóc?	How may I help you?
Czy macie . . .?	Do you have . . .?
rzeczy osobiste	personal belongings

OBJAŚNIENIA

EXPLANATORY NOTES

To jest mój bagaż
   moja walizka
   moja torba

This is my baggage
   suitcase
   handbag

EXERCISES

1. Copy the text, read it aloud, and translate it.

2. Translate into Polish:
   Where is the customs? I have nothing to declare. This is not new.
   Is this duty-free? May I go now?

ZAPAMIĘTAJ

REMEMBER

Gdzie jest odprawa celna?	Where is the customs?
Nie mam nic do oclenia.	I have nothing to declare.
To nie jest nowe.	This is not new.
Czy to jest wolne od cła?	Is this duty-free?
Czy jest w pobliżu stacja benzynowa?	Is there a gasoline pump around here?
Gdzie jest warsztat samochodowy?	Where can I find a garage?
Mam przebitą oponę.	I have a flat tire.
Czy może mi pan naprawić oponę?	Will you please repair this tire?
Ile to będzie kosztować?	How much will the work cost?
Kiedy będzie gotowe?	When will it be ready?

GRAMMAR

PERSONAL PRONOUNS

Note: The cases are explained in the Grammar part of Lesson 3.

Singular

Nom.	**ja** - I	**ty** - you	**on** - he	**ona** - she	**ono** - it
Gen.	mnie - mię	ciebie - cię	jego- go	jej	jego -go
Dat.	mnie - mi	tobie - ci	jemu- mu	jej - niej	jemu - mu
Acc.	mnie - mię	ciebie - cię	jego - go	ją - nią	je - nie
Instr.	mną	tobą	nim	nią	nim
Loc.	o mnie	o tobie	o nim	o niej	o nim

Plural

Nom:	**my**- we	**wy** - you	**oni**- they	**one** - they	**one** -they
Gen.	nas	was	ich-nich	ich-nich	ich-nich
Dat.	nam	wam	im-nim	im-nim	im-nim
Acc.	nas	was	ich-nich	je-nie	je-nie
Instr.	nami	wami	nimi	nimi	nimi
Loc.	o nas	o was	o nich	o nich	o nich

In both the singular and plural, more than one form occurs in the genitive, dative and accusative. The forms beginning with **n**-are used after prepositions, and the remaining forms are used in all other cases. The short forms, **ci, cię, go, mi, mu** do not have independent stress.

EXERCISES

1. Translate into English.
   A ty? Ona czyta gazetę. Znam je. Nie znam ich.

2. Translate into Polish.
   Where is Joseph? Have you seen him? Yes, he was here. Where is he now?

REFLEXIVE PRONOUNS

Nom. -
Gen. siebie - się (myself)
Dat. sobie
Acc. siebie - się
Inst. sobą
Loc. o sobie

Reflexive pronouns can be applied to any of three persons, thus representing 'myself', 'thyself', 'himself', 'herself', 'itself', 'ourselves', 'yourselves', 'themselves'.

Examples: Widzę siebie w lustrze.
　　　　　I can see myself in the mirror.

EXERCISE

3. Translate into Polish.
    She poured herself some tea. They are always pleased with themselves.

LEKCJA TRZECIA

TRANSPORT LOKALNY

TAKSÓWKA

Józef: Gdzie jest postój taksówek?

Portier: Jest tam, na lewo.

Kierowca: Gdzie pan jedzie?

Józef: Na Żoliborz. Tu są nasze bagaże.

Kierowca: To się nie zmieści do bagażnika. Muszę włożyć coś na dach.

Józef: Nareszcie w domu! Ile się należy?

Kierowca: 15 złotych.

Józef: Proszę, reszta dla pana.

Kierowca: Dziękuję bardzo. Do widzenia!

Józef: Dziękuję!

LESSON THREE

LOCAL TRANSPORTATION

TAXI

Józef:	Where is the taxi stop?
Porter:	It's over there, on the left.
T. Driver:	Where are you going?
Józef:	Żoliborz. Here's our luggage.
T. Driver:	It won't fit in the trunk I'll have to put some on the roof.
Józef:	Finally home! How much do I owe you?
T. Driver:	15 zlotys.
Józef:	Here you go and keep the change!
T. Driver:	Thanks a lot. Good-bye!
Józef:	Thank you!

VOCABULARY

bagażnik	trunk
bagaż	luggage
dach	roof
dom	home
do widzenia	good-bye
jechać	go
lewo	left
na	on
należeć (posiadać)	own
postój taksówki	taxi stop
reszta	change
są	are
taksówka	taxi
tu	here
to	it
włożyć	put
w	in
w końcu	finally
zatrzymać	keep
złoty	Polish currency

ZWROTY

Ile to kosztuje?
Ile kosztuje taksówka
    na lotnisko?
Proszę zanieść mój bagaż
    na postój taksówek.

EXPRESSIONS

How much?
How much does the taxi to
    the airport cost?
Take my baggage to a
    taxi stand.

OBJAŚNIENIA

Gdzie jest
    północ?
    południe?
    wschód?
    zachód?

EXPLANATORY NOTES

Which way is
    North?
    South?
    East?
    West?

EXERCISES

1. Copy the text, read it aloud and translate it.

2. Translate into Polish:
    Where is the airport? How much does a taxi to the airport
        cost? Which way is North? What is the name of this place?

ZAPAMIĘTAJ

REMEMBER

Jak się nazywa ta miejscowość?   What is the name of this place?
Dokąd prowadzi ta droga?   Where does this road lead to?
Ile jest kilometrów stąd do   How many kilometers is it to
  Warszawy?   Warsaw?

GRAMMAR

NOUNS

There is **no article,** either definite or indefinite in the Polish language; book may mean equally well 'the book', 'a book' or simply 'book'. This peculiarity of the Polish language does not present any difficulty to the student, as it is always clear from the context whether 'book', 'a book' or 'the book' is meant.

Genders

There are **three** genders in Polish: **Masculine, Feminine and Neuter.** The gender of noun is indicated by the termination of its Nominative Singular case (see Cases below):

masculine are - most nouns ending in a consonant in the Nom.Sing.
feminine are   - nouns ending in -**a, -i**
neuter are   - nouns ending in -**o, -e, -ę**.

It is necessary to know the gender of a noun to be able to select the correct form of an adjective or pronoun which is to be used in conjunction with it.

Cases

There are **seven 'cases'** in Polish:
Nominative, Genitive, Dative, Accusative, Instrumental, Locative and Vocative.

The **Nominative**   answers the question: **who? what?**
      (English subject)

The **Genitive**   answers the question: **whose? of whom? of what?**
      (English 'possessive')

The **Dative**   answers the question: **to whom? to what?**
      (English 'indirect object')

The **Accusative**   answers the question: **whom? what?**
      (English 'direct object')

The **Instrumental** answers question: **by** or **with whom? by** or **with what?**

The **Locative**   answers the question: **about whom?** or **about what?** and is always preceded by a preposition such as *w* (in), *na* (on), *o* (about), *przy* (next to), *po* (after), i.e., in a sentence answers a question: **where?**

The **Vocative**   is the case-form used when addressing a person or
                              thing.

Examples: What is that?   That is a/the table.
                  Co to jest?   To jest stół.

EXERCISE

1. Translate into Polish.
   Who is that? That is a/the picture. That is a/the table, and that is
   a/the desk. Where is a/the student?

LEKCJA CZWARTA

HOTEL

PRZYBYCIE

Jan: Dobry wieczór. Nazywam się Jan Kowalski. Mam zarezerwowany pokój dwuosobowy.

Recep: Tak, rzeczywiście. Proszę wypełnić te formularze. Będę również potrzebował oba paszporty.

Jan: Proszę bardzo.

Recep: Dziękuję. Tu są klucze, pokój numer 214. Portier pomoże państwu zanieść bagaże.

Jan: Gdzie możemy zaparkować samochód?

Recep: Na parkingu hotelowym, z tyłu budynku.

OBSŁUGA

Ewa: O której godzinie podawane jest śniadanie?

Recep: Śniadanie można zjeść w naszej restauracji od 6-tej do 11-tej rano. Podajemy również do pokoju.

Jan: Jakie inne usługi oferujecie?

Recep: Mamy kantor wymiany walut i pocztę tu obok, w hallu, jak również fryzjera i trzy sklepy z upominkami. Basen kąpielowy znajduje się w podziemiu.

LESSON FOUR

HOTEL

CHECK-IN

Jan: Good evening. My name is Jan Kowalski. I have a reservation for a double room.

Clerk: Yes, here it is. Please fill out these forms. And I will need both your passports.

Jan: Here you go.

Clerk: Thank you. Here are your keys, room number 214. A porter will help you with your luggage.

Jan: Where can we park our car?

Clerk: In the hotel parking lot, in the back of the building.

SERVICE

Ewa: At what time is breakfast served?

Clerk: Our restaurant is open for breakfast from 6 to 11 A.M. Room service is available as well.

Jan: What other services do you offer?

Clerk: There is an exchange counter and a post office right here in the lobby, along with a hairdresser and three gift shops. The swimming pool is in the basement.

VOCABULARY

będę	I will
do	to
formularz	form
godzina	hour
klucze	keys
który (której)	which
oba	both
obsługa	service
od	from
podziemie	basement
pokój	room
portier	porter
poczta	post
rano	morning
restauracja	restaurant
recepcja	lobby, reception room
śniadanie	breakfast
sklep	shop
trzy	three
upominek	gift
usługi	services
wasze	your
wymiana	exchange
zaparkować	park
zjeść	eat

ZWROTY

EXPRESSIONS

Czy masz?	Do you have?
Tak jest/zgadza się	That's right
Państwo Kowalscy	Mr. & Mrs. Kowalski

OBJAŚNIENIA

EXPLANATORY NOTES

hotel	hotel
pensjonat	pension
pokój jednoosobowy	single room
dwuosobowy	double room
pokój z łazienką	room with bathroom
pokojowa	room maid

EXERCISES

1. Copy the text, read aloud, and translate it.

2. Translate into Polish:
   Where is the hotel? I want a key to my room. Please call a taxi.
   Here is my address. I am leaving tomorrow.

ZAPAMIĘTAJ	REMEMBER
Jaka jest cena za dobę?	What is the price per day?
tydzień ?	week?
miesiąc?	month?
Czy jest pokój z łazienką lub	Do you have a room with bath
prysznicem?	or shower?
Czy są pokoje z klimatyzacją?	Do you have an air-conditioned
	room?
Proszę o lepszy pokój.	I want a better room.
Proszę o gorącą wodę.	I want hot water
-wodę z lodem.	-ice water
-lód.	-ice
-poduszkę.	-pillow
-ręcznik.	-towel
-mydło.	-soap
-papier toaletowy.	-toilet paper
-jeszcze jeden koc.	-another blanket
Proszę mnie obudzić o 6-ej rano.	Please wake me up at 6 A.M.
Proszę dać te rzeczy do prania.	Please have these clothes washed.
Kiedy je dostanę z powrotem?	When can I have them back?
Chcę porozmawiać z	I want to speak to the manager.
kierownikiem.	
Poproszę o rachunek.	May I have my bill please?

53

GRAMMAR

DECLENSION OF NOUNS

Inflected nouns, adjectives and pronounce are said to be "declined" and a method of their inflection is called their "declension". This word is also used to denote the main groups into which nouns and adjectives are divided.

Masculine nouns ending in a consonant

Singular

Nom.	koń	horse	pan	gentleman
Gen.	konia		pana	
Dat.	koniowi		panu	
Acc.	konia		pana	
Instr.	koniem		panem	
Loc.	o koniu		o panu	
Voc.	koniu!		panie!	

Plural

Nom.	konie		panowie	
Gen.	koni		panów	
Dat.	koniom		panom	
Acc.	konie		panów	
Inst.	końmi		panami	
Loc.	o koniach		o panach	
Voc.	konie!		panowie!	

Most masculine nouns form the plural by adding - **i** - **e** or **y**, while the ending - **owie** is found with nouns denoting status, profession or family relationship.

Masculine nouns ending in - **a** are declined in the singular as feminine nouns ending in **a** and in the plural as the masculine nouns ending in a consonant.

Feminine nouns

Singular

Nom.	córka	daughter	pani	lady
Gen.	córki		pani	
Dat.	córce		pani	
Acc.	córkę		panią	
Instr.	córką		panią	
Loc.	o córce		o pani	
Voc.	córko!		pani!	

Plural

Nom.	córki	panie
Gen.	córek	pań
Dat.	córkom	paniom
Acc.	córki	panie
Instr.	córkami	paniami
Loc.	o córkach	o paniach
Voc.	córki!	panie!

EXERCISES

1. Give the different cases of the masculine nouns: Polak, student both in singular and plural.

2. Give the different cases of the feminine nouns: woda, wieś both in singular and plural.

LEKCJA PIĄTA

PYTANIE O KIERUNEK

Jan i Ewa zdecydowali się wyjść do miasta.

Jan: Może nie powinniśmy wychodzić wieczorem, zgubimy się.

Ewa: Nie, znamy miasto zupełnie dobrze, chodź.

Parę godzin później.

Jan: A jednak, zgubiliśmy się.

Ewa: Spytajmy o drogę w kawiarni.

Jan: Przepraszam, czy może pan/pani mi powiedzieć, jak trafić do Hotelu Victoria?

Kelner: To jest bardzo daleko. Muszą państwo pojechać tramwajem.

Ewa: Którym?

Kelner: Trzynastką. Przystanek jest za rogiem na lewo.

Jan: Dziękuję. Dobranoc.

LESSON FIVE

ASKING FOR DIRECTIONS

Jan and Ewa decide to go out on the town.

Jan: May be we shouldn't be going out at night, we'll get lost!

Ewa: No, we know the city well enough. Come on.

A few hours later.

Jan: Well, we are lost.

Ewa: Let's go ask in that cafe.

Jan: Excuse me. Could you tell me how to get to the Hotel Victoria?

Waiter: Oh, you are quite far away. You should take a tram.

Ewa: Which one?

Waiter: Number 13. The stop is around the corner, on the left.

Jan: Thank you. Good night.

VOCABULARY

chodź	come
daleko	far away
dobranoc	good night
jednak	after all
jesteście	you are
kawiarnia	cafe, coffee shop
miasto	town
może	maybe
nie powinniśmy	we shoudn't
parę	few
powiedzieć	tell
powinniście	you should
pojechać (tramwajem)	to go, to take a tram
później	later
przystanek	stop
trafić	to get to
tramwaj	tram
trzynaście	thirteen
spytać się (pytać się) ask	
zdecydować się	decide
zgubić się	get lost
zupełnie dobrze	well enough
wyjść	go out

ZWROTY

EXPRESSIONS

zupełnie dobrze	well enough
niedaleko	not very far
bardzo daleko stąd	very far from here

OBJAŚNIENIA

EXPLANATORY NOTES

Czy może mi pan/pani
  powiedzieć, gdzie jest...?
To jest tam na prawo/na lewo
Proszę iść do...potem skręcić
  w lewo/w pierwszą przecznicę
  na lewo.

Can you tell me where is...?

It's there on the right/left
Go to...then turn left/take
  the first turning
  on the left.

EXERCISES

1. Copy the text, read it aloud and translate it.

2. Translate into Polish:
   Where is...? How far is it from here to ...? It's not far. What is this place? This way.

ZAPAMIĘTAJ	REMEMBER
Dokąd prowadzi ta droga?	Where does this road lead to?
Przepraszam, zabłądziłem.	Excuse me, I am lost.
Czy może pan mi pomóc?	Can you help me?
Czy ma pan mapę?	Have you a map?
Czy może mi pan/pani wskazać drogę?	Can you guide me?
Proszę pokazać.	Please point.
Jak się nazywa ta ulica?	What is the name of this street?
Proszę skręcić w prawo.	Turn right.
Proszę skręcić w lewo.	Turn left.
tam	there
tutaj	here
w pobliżu	near
daleko	far
niedaleko	not very far
bardzo daleko stąd	very far from here
w tym kierunku	this way

GRAMMAR

DECLENSION OF NOUNS

Neuter nouns

Singular

Nom.	niebo	sky, heaven	ćwiczenie	exercise
Gen.	nieba		ćwiczenia	
Dat.	niebu		ćwiczeniu	
Acc.	niebo		ćwiczenie	
Instr.	niebem		ćwiczeniem	
Loc.	o niebie		o ćwiczeniu	
Voc.	niebo!		ćwiczenie!	

Plural

Nom.	nieba		ćwiczenia
Ge.	nieb		ćwiczeń
Dat.	niebom		ćwiczeniom
Acc.	nieba		ćwiczenia
Instr.	niebami		ćwiczeniami
Loc.	o niebach		o ćwiczeniach
Voc.	nieba!		ćwiczenia!

DIMINUTIVES

A characteristic feature of Polish nouns is their capability of forming diminutives, e.g.: kapelusz (hat) - kapelusik. Apart from expressing relative size, they are used in family life, e.g.: matka (mother) - mama, mamusia as well as in Christian names with reference to young people e.g.: Jan-Jaś, Barbara- Basia.

EXERCISE

1. Give the different cases of the neuter nouns: lato - summer, ramię - arm both in the singular and plural.

LEKCJA SZÓSTA

W RESTAURACJI

Jan: Halo, czy mogę mówić z panem Urbaniakiem?

Józef.   Przy telefonie.

Jan: Mówi Jan Kowalski, poznaliśmy się w samolocie.

Józef: Oczywiście! Pamiętam!

Jan: Chcielibyśmy zaprosić państwa w piątek na obiad.

Józef: Z przyjemnością przyjdziemy.

Jan: Spotkajmy się w Hotelu Victoria o 8-ej wieczorem.

Józef: Wspaniale, do zobaczenia.

Piątek. W restauracji.

Kelner: Czy państwo mogą już zamówić?

Jan: Tak. Mario, co dla ciebie?

Maria: Poproszę o rosół i kotlet z dzika.

Ewa: Ja wezmę zupę szczawiową i sarninę.

Jan: Józefie, zamawiaj.

Józef: Dla mnie flaki i pieczona gęś.

Kelner: A pan?

Jan: Ja wezmę ozór wołowy na zimno a potem filet cielęcy.

Kelner: Czy podać coś do picia?

Jan: Możemy zamówić butelkę czerwonego wytrawnego wina?

61

Kelner: Oczywiście.

Józef: Był to wspaniały obiad! Dziękujemy bardzo!

Jan: Było nam bardzo miło. Kelner, czy mogę prosić o rachunek?

Kelner: Proszę bardzo.

Jan: Czy mogę zapłacić VISĄ?

Kelner: Oczywiście.

Jan: Proszę bardzo.

Kelner: Dziękuję . Dobranoc!

LESSON SIX

AT THE RESTAURANT

Jan: Hello, may I please speak to Mr. Urbaniak?

Józef: This is him.

Jan: This is Jan Kowalski. We met on the plane.

Józef: Of course! I remember.

Jan: We would like to invite you and your wife to dinner next Friday.

Józef: We would love to come!

Jan: Let's meet at the Hotel Victoria at 8 P.M.

Józef: Wonderful! See you then!

Friday, at the restaurant.

Waiter: Are you ready to order?

Jan: Yes. Maria, go ahead.

Maria: Could I please have the broth and the boar?

Ewa: I will have the sorrel soup and the venison.

Jan: Józef, go ahead.

Józef: Could I have the tripe and the roast goose?

Waiter: And you sir?

Jan: I'll have the cold beef tongue and then the veal scallop.

Waiter: Anything to drink?

Jan: Could we have a bottle of dry red wine?

Waiter: Certainly.

Józef: That was a wonderful meal. Thank you very much.

Jan: It was our pleasure. Waiter! Could we please have the bill?

Waiter: Here you go.

Jan: Can I pay by VISA?

Waiter: Of course.

Jan: Here you go.

Waiter: Thank you. Good evening!

VOCABULARY

ciebie	you
cielęcina	veal
butelka	bottle
dzik	boar
filet	scallop
flaki	tripe
gotowy	ready
język	tongue
jedzenie	meal
kelner	waiter
mówić	speak
na	for, on, upon, at, by, in
obiad	dinner
oczywiście	certainly/of course
płacić	pay
picie	drink
pan	sir
pieczone	roasted
pamiętać	remember
poznać	meet
rosół	broth
rachunek	bill
samolot	airplane/plane
szczaw	sorrel
sarnina	venison
wspaniale	wonderful
wytrawne	dry
wino	wine
wołowe	beef
zamówienie	order

ZWROTY — EXPRESSIONS

ZWROTY	EXPRESSIONS
Czy mogę?	May I ?
Chciałbym...	I would like...
Spotkajmy się	Let's meet
Czy mogę prosić o...?	Could I please have...?
Czy państwo mogą już zamówić?	Are you ready to order?
Przy telefonie.	This is him.
Czy mogę prosić o rachunek?	Could I please have the bill?
Było nam miło.	It was our pleasure.
To było.	That was.

Proszę kartę.	Here's the menu.
Proszę podać mi kartę.	May I see the menu?
bar mleczny	milk bar
Obiad wart był tego.	The dinner was worth it.
Ciemne czy jasne piwo?	Dark or light beer?

EXERCISES

1. Copy the text, read it aloud, and translate it.

2. Translate into Polish:
   It was our pleasure. Are you ready to order? Could I please have the veal scallop?

ZAPAMIĘTAJ

REMEMBER

Gdzie jest dobra restauracja?	Where is a good restaurant?
Proszę mi przynieść filiżankę	Please bring me a cup
szklankę	a glass
widelec	a fork
nóż	a knife
łyżkę	a spoon
talerz	a plate
herbatę	tea
pieprz	pepper
sól	salt
cukier	sugar
ocet	vinegar
chleb i masło	bread and butter

GRAMMAR

VERBS

The Polish verb has only three tenses:
present, past, future
There are two main aspects of verbs:
imperfective (imp) and perfective (pf)

A verb in the **imperfective aspect** denotes on action of an incomplete or indefinite character, a continued action or one which is actually in progress at the time of speaking, without regard to its beginning or end or results. This aspect has three tenses:
Present tense   **Past** tense   **Future** tense

A verb in the **perfective aspect** describes on action which has been or will be definitely completed. It therefore can not have a present tense, but only a past tense and future tense.

Present Tense

iść - to go   **czytać** - to read   **wiedzieć** - know

Singular

ja idę	czytam	wiem	I
ty idziesz	czytasz	wiesz	you
on, ona, ono idzie	czyta	wie	he, she, it

Plural

my idziemy	czytamy	wiemy	we
wy idziecie	czytacie	wiecie	you
oni, one idą	czytają	wiedzą	they

EXERCISE

1. Give the conjugation of two verbs in the Present Tense: robię - I do, piszę - I write, both in the singular and plural.

LEKCJA SIÓDMA

ZAKUPY

Jan i Ewa udali się na zakupy na Stare Miasto.

Sklep z wyrobami skórzanymi.

Sprzedawca: Czym mogę służyć?

Ewa: Dziękuję, tylko rozglądam się.

Jan: Patrz na te torby, są piękne. Myślisz, że Elżbiecie by się podobały?

Ewa: Bardzo by się jej podobały. Przepraszam pana!

Sprzedawca: Tak?

Ewa: Czy mogę obejrzeć tę torbę na lewo?

Sprzedawca: Oczywiście. Proszę.

Ewa: Ile kosztuje?

Sprzedawca: 25 złotych.

Ewa: Wezmę ją. Czy akceptujecie karty kredytowe?

Sprzedawca: Tak.

Spacerując, para zdecydowała się wejść do apteki.

Jan: Potrzebuję jakiegoś lekarstwa przeciwko kaszlowi.

Farmaceuta: Mamy dużo różnych syropów i pastylek. Czy ma pan też katar?

Jan: Tak, mam rzeczywiście.

Farmaceuta:	W tym przypadku zalecam to.
Jan:	Czy potrzebna jest recepta?
Farmaceuta:	Nie jest potrzebna. Czy może jeszcze coś?
Jan:	Witaminę C w tabletkach.
Farmaceuta:	Proszę.

Ewa chce kupić palto na zimę. Zatrzymują się w małym butiku.

Ewa:	Czy może pan pokazać mi, gdzie są zimowe palta?
Sprzedawca:	W tyle sklepu, po prawej stronie. Czy szuka pani czegoś specjalnego?
Ewa:	Tak, długiego wełnianego palta, odpornego na deszcz.
Sprzedawca:	Jaki numer/rozmiar pani nosi?
Ewa:	38.
Sprzedawca:	Jaki chce pani kolor?
Ewa:	Beżowy lub brązowy. Czarny lub granat może być też.
Sprzedawca:	Jak ten?
Ewa:	Podoba mi się, czy mogę przymierzyć?

LESSON SEVEN

SHOPPING

Jan and Ewa go shopping in the Old Town.

Leather Goods Store.

Salesperson: Can I help you?

Ewa: I'm just looking around, thank you.

Jan: Look at these bags. They are beautiful! Do you think Elizabeth might like one?

Ewa: She would love it! Excuse me, miss!

Salesperson: Yes?

Ewa: Could I please have a look at that bag on the left?

Salesperson: Certainly. Here you go.

Ewa: How much is it?

Salesperson: 25 zlotys.

Ewa: I'll take it. Do you accept credit cards?

Salesperson: Yes we do.

Walking along, the couple decides to stop in a pharmacy.

Jan: I need some cough medicine.

Pharmacist: We have several different syrups and pills. Do you have a cold too?

Jan: Yes, I do in fact.

Pharmacist:	Then, I recommend this.
Jan:	Do I need a prescription?
Pharmacist:	No, that is not necessary. Can I get you anything else?
Jan:	Some vitamin C tablets please.
Pharmacist:	Here you go.

Ewa needs to buy a winter coat. They stop at a small boutique.

Ewa:	Could you please show me where the overcoats are?
Salesperson:	In the back of the store, on the right hand side. Are you looking for something in particular?
Ewa:	Yes a long wool coat that is waterproof.
Salesperson:	What size do you wear?
Ewa:	38
Salesperson:	And what color are you looking for?
Ewa:	Beige or brown. Black or navy would be fine too.
Salesperson:	How about this one?
Ewa:	I like it. Could I try it on?

Kupowanie odzieży

Shopping for clothing

szlafrok	bath robe
pasek	belt
bluzka	blouse
stanik	bra
płaszcz/palto	coat
sukienka	dress
futro	fur coat
rękawiczki	gloves
chusteczka	handkerchief
kapelusz	hat
marynarka	jacket
dżinsy	jeans
bielizna	lingerie
krawat	tie
spodnie	trousers
pidżama	pajamas
sandały	sandals
buty	shoes
koszula	shirt
spódnica	skirt
skarpetki	socks
kostium kąpielowy	swim suit
pończochy	panty-hose
garnitur (men's)	suit
kostium (women's)	suit
rajstopy	tights
tenisówki	tennis shoes

Kolory

Colors

biały	white
beżowy	beige
czerwony	red
czrny	black
fioletowy	purple
niebieski	blue
pomarańczowy	orange
srebrny	silver
szary	grey
zielony	green
złoty	gold
różowy	pink

Kupowanie żywności

Shopping for food

Czy można dostać

Do you have

jabłka?	apples?
banany?	bananas?
fasolę?	beans?
befsztyk?	steak?
piwo?	beer?
chleb?	bread?
masło?	butter?
kapustę?	cabbage?
tort?	cake?
cukierki?	candy?
ser?	cheese?
kurczaki?	chicken?
czekoladę?	chocolate?
kawę?	coffee?
śmietankę?	cream?
mleko?	milk?
wodę?	water?

VOCABULARY

akceptować	accept
apteka	pharmacy
beż	beige
brązowy	brown
deszcz	rain
długie	long
granat	navy
gdzie	where
katar	cold
kaszel	cough
kolor	color
kochać/lubić	love
lekarstwo	medicine
mały	small
nie	no
nieprzemakalny	waterproof
obejrzeć	have a look
odporne	resistant
pani	Mrs.
panienka	Miss
piękne	beautiful
patrzeć	look
potrzebować	need
pokazać	show
palto	coat/overcoat
rozmiar/numer	size
syrop	syrups
sklep	shop
skóra	leather
spacerując	walking along
tak	yes
torba	bag
też	too
także	also
tabletki	pills
tył	back
udać się	go
wziąć	take
witaminy	vitamins
wyroby	good
zapłacić	pay

zakupy	shopping
zatrzymać	stop
zdecydować	decide
zima	winter

ZWROTY

EXPRESSIONS

szukać czegoś	look for something
będzie dobry	would be fine
W czym mogę pomóc?	How can I help you?
rozglądać się	looking around
Ile to kosztuje?	How much is it?
z prawej strony	right hand side

OBJAŚNIENIA

EXPLANATORY NOTES

Gdzie można kupić...?	Where can one buy...?
jeśli chcesz kupić	if you wish to buy
coś eleganckiego	something smart/elegant
zbyt jaskrawy	too showy
coś w spokojnym kolorze	some quiet color

EXERCISES

1. Copy the text, read it aloud and translate it.

2. Translate into Polish:
   Let us go in. I'll take it. How can I help you? Do you accept credit cards? She would love it.

ZAPAMIĘTAJ

REMEMBER

sprzedaje się	is (are) sold
stać w kolejce	waiting in line
nic nie kupuję	I buy nothing

GRAMMAR

VERBS

As the verb changes its form in the process of conjugation the personal pronoun is usually left out.

Past Tense

This is formed by adding to the past participle the past tense endings of the verb **być** - to be, which vary according to number and gender.

Singular

iść - to go		**czytać-** to read	
M	**F**	**M**	**F**
ja szedłem	szłam	czytałem	czytałam
ty szedłeś	szłaś	czytałeś	czytałaś
on szedł		czytał	
ona	szła		czytała
ono szło - **N**		czytało - **N**	

The past participle is formed by replacing the infinitive ending - **ć** with the suffix - **ł** for masculine gender, **-ła** for feminine, **ło** - for neuter.

Plural

M	**F**	**M**	**F**
my szliśmy	szłyśmy	czytaliśmy	czytałyśmy
wy szliście	szłyście	czytaliście	czytałyście
oni szli		czytali	
one	szły		czytały

EXERCISE

1. Give the conjugation of the verbs robię - I do, piszę - I write in the Past Tense, both in the singular and plural.

LEKCJA ÓSMA

POCZTA

Józef i Maria wysyłają list do przyjaciół w Stanach Zjednoczonych.

Józef: W którym okienku kupię znaczki?

Urzędnik: Numer 5.

Józef: Czy mogę dostać 10 znaczków lotniczych do Stanów Zjednoczonych?

Urzędnik: Proszę. Czy to wszystko?

Józef: Czy może mi pan powiedzieć, ile kosztuje wysłanie paczki lotniczej?

Urzędnik: 1,50 złotych za wszystko do 10 kilogramów.

Józef: Jak długo idzie przesyłka?

Urzędnik: Około dwóch tygodni.

LESSON EIGHT

POST OFFICE

Józef and Maria mail a letter to their friends in the USA.

Józef: What window do I go to for stamps?

Clerk: Number 5

Józef: Could I please get 10 air mail stamps for the USA.

Clerk: Here you go. Is that all?

Józef: Could you also tell me how much does it cost to send a package airmail.

Clerk: It is 1.50 zlotys for anything up to 10 kilos.

Józef: How long does it usually take?

Clerk: About 2 weeks.

VOCABULARY

ich	their
kosztuje	cost
list	letter
lotnicza	airmail
okienko	window
około	about
paczka	package
powiedz	tell
także	also
wysłać	send/mail
wszystko	anything/everything
znaczki	stamps

ZWROTY

EXPRESSIONS

Czy to wszystko?	Is that all?
Ile?	How much?
Jak długo?	How long?

OBJAŚNIENIA

EXPLANATORY NOTES

Chcę to wysłać — I want to send this
    jako przesyłkę poleconą — registered
    pocztą lotniczą — air mail
    jako expres — special delivery/express
    jako paczkę — parcel
    z ubezpieczniem — insured

EXERCISES

1. Copy the text, read it aloud, and translate it.

2. Translate into Polish:
   May I have some postage stamps? Where is the post office?
   How much is the postage on this lettter? Letters for abroad.

ZAPAMIĘTAJ	REMEMBER
Ta paczka zawiera	This package contains
książki	books
słodycze	candy
zabawki	toys
żywność	food
odzież	clothing
rzeczy osobiste	personal belongings
przedmioty łatwo psujące się	perishable food
przedmioty łatwo tłukące się	fragile material

GRAMMAR

VERBS

Future Tense

The simple future tense is formed by adding the perfective aspect to the present tense of the verb, i.e., **czytać** , impf., **prze**czytać, pf. - to read; ja czytam, present tense - I am reading; ja przeczytam, future tense - I shall read.

Singular

iść - to go	**czytać** - to read	**wiedzieć**- to know
ja pójdę	**prze**czytam	**będę** wiedział
ty pójdziesz	**prze**czytasz	**będziesz** wiedział
on pójdzie	**prze**czyta	**będzie** wiedział
ona pójdzie	**prze**czyta	**będzie** wiedziała
ono pójdzie	**prze**czyta	**będzie** wiedziało

Plural

my pójdziemy	**prze**czytamy	**będziemy** wiedzieli
wy pójdziecie	**prze**czytacie	**będziecie** wiedzieli
oni pójdą	**prze**czytają	**będą** wiedzieli
one pójdą	**prze**czytają	**będą** wiedziały

The future imperfective aspect is a compound tense formed by combining the active past participle or infinitive of the verb with the future of the auxiliary verb **być** - to be, which runs as follows:

Sg. będę	I shall be	**Pl.** będziemy	we shall be
będziesz	you will be	będziecie	you will be
będzie	he, she, it will	będą	they will be

EXERCISE

1. Give the conjugation of the verbs robię - I do, piszę - I write in Future Tense, both in the singular and plural.

LEKCJA DZIEWIĄTA

BĘDĄC GOŚCIEM

Józef i Maria zaprosili Jana i Ewę do domu.

Józef: Chcielibyśmy zaprosić was do nas na obiad we wtorek wieczorem.

Jan: Bardzo nam przyjemnie, przyjdziemy. Gdzie mieszkacie? (*Józef tłumaczy, jak się dostać do ich domu.*)

W domu.

Józef: Prosimy.

Jan: Tu jest coś małego dla ciebie. (*wręcza mu butelkę*)

Ewa: A to jest dla ciebie, Mario. (*wręcza jej kwiatki*)

Józef: Niepotrzebnie. Dziękujemy. Siadajcie. Czego się napijecie?

Jan: Dla mnie cokolwiek.

Józef: Coś dobrego! Ewo, co dla ciebie?

Ewa: Dla mnie trochę vermutu, dziękuję. (*idzie do kuchni*)
Mario, czy mogę ci w czymś pomóc?

Maria: Nie, dziękuję, wszystko zrobione. Proszę do stołu.

Po obiedzie dwie pary rozmawiają przy kawie.

Ewa: To było wspaniałe, Mario, świetnie gotujesz.

Maria: Dziękuję, Janie, spróbuj kawałek tego tortu orzechowego.

Jan: Wygląda wspaniale, ale już więcej nie mogę.

Maria: Proszę, dam ci mały kawałek.

Jan: To jest mały?

LESSON NINE

BEING A GUEST

Józef and Maria invite Jan and Ewa to their house.

Józef: We would like to invite you over for dinner next Tuesday night.

Jan: We'd love to come. Where do you live? (*Józef explains how to get to his house*).

At the house.
Józef: Come in!

Jan: Here is a little something for you. (*hands him bottle*)

Ewa: And these are for you Maria. (*hands her flowers*).

Józef: You shouldn't have. Thank you very much. Have a seat. What would you like to drink?

Jan: I'll have whatever you're having.

Józef: Something good! Ewa, and for you?

Ewa: I'll just have some vermouth, thank you. (*goes into kitchen*) Maria, can I help you with anything?

Maria: No, thank you, everything is done. Please come to the table.

After meal, the two couples are chatting over coffee.
Ewa: That was absolutely wonderful. Maria, you are an excellent cook!

Maria: Oh, not at all, Jan, try a piece of this walnut torte.

Jan: I'm so full... but it looks so delicious.

Maria: Here, I will give you a small piece...

Jan: That's small?

VOCABULARY

absolutnie	absolutely
bardzo dobre	excellent
coś	something
gotować	cook
cokolwiek	whatever
czego	what
dostać	get
gdzie	where
gość	guest
dom	house
kawa	coffee
kawałek	piece
kuchnia	kitchen
kwiatki	flower
mały	small
mieszkać	live
obiad	dinner
przy (kawie/herbacie)	over (a cup of coffee/tea)
pełny	full
pomóc	help
próbować	try
rozmawiać/gawędzić	chat
smaczne	delicious
stół	table
tu	here
tłumaczyć	explain
wszystko	everything
wieczór	evening

ZWROTY

EXPRESSIONS

Chcielibyśmy zaprosić was do nas na obiad.	We would like to invite you over for dinner.
Gdzie mieszkacie?	Where do you live?
dla ciebie	for you
usiądźcie	have a seat
Czego się napijecie?	What would you like to drink?

OBJAŚNIENIA

po prawej stronie	on the right hand (side)
co mam panu podać	what (shall-can) I serve you with?
nie jadam	I can't eat

EXPLANATORY NOTES

EXERCISES

1. Copy the text, read it aloud, and translate it.

2. Translate into Polish:
   What will you have for dinner? What would you like to drink?
   Would you please come to my house on Sunday? Please come
   again.

ZAPAMIĘTAJ

REMEMBER

proszę wejść	please come in
proszę usiąść	please be seated
Może pan coś zje?	May I offer you something to eat?
Czy lubi pan herbatę?	Do you like tea?
Do widzenia, było mi naprawdę bardzo miło.	Good-bye, I had a delightful time

GRAMMAR

REFLEXIVE VERBS

The reflexive verbs consist of verbs followed immediately by the
reflexive pronoun **się.** They are conjugated according to the normal
patterns with **się** remaining unchanged throughout.

Singular
bawić się - enjoy oneself   **myć się** - wash oneself

ja   bawię się   myję się
ty   bawisz się   myjesz się
on bawi się   myje się
ona bawi się   myje się
ono bawi się   myje się

Plural

my bawimy się   myjemy się
wy bawicie się   myjecie się
oni bawią się   myją się
one bawią się   myją się

AUXILLIARY VERB

Polish has only one auxilliary verb **być -** to be.   Its conjugation is
irregular.

Present Tense

Positive		**Negative**	
I am	**ja jestem**	I am not	**ja nie jestem**
you are	**ty jesteś**	you are not	**ty nie jesteś**
he is	**on jest**	he is not	**on nie jest**
she is	**ona jest**	she is not	**ona nie jest**
it is	**ono jest**	it is not	**ono nie jest**
we are	**my jesteśmy**	we are not	**my nie jesteśmy**
you are	**wy jesteście**	you are not	**wy nie jesteście**
they are	**oni są**	they are not	**oni nie są M**
	one są		**one nie są F&N**

EXERCISE

1. Give the conjugation of the reflexive verbs: śmiać się - to laugh,
   czesać się - to comb, both in the singular and plural.

LEKCJA DZIESIĄTA

OPIEKA LEKARSKA

Po powrocie do hotelu, Jan poczuł się źle.

Ewa: Mówiłam ci, że nie powinieneś jeść tego trzeciego kawałka ciasta.

Jan: Za późno. Czuję się okropnie!

Ewa: Musimy zawołać lekarza. Zadzwonię do recepcji i poproszę o pomoc.

Wykręca numer.

Ewa: Tak, mówi Ewa Kowalska z pokoju 214. Mój mąż czuje się źle i potrzebuje lekarza.

Recep: Mogę to załatwić. Czy chciałaby pani, aby przyszedł do pokoju?

Ewa: Tak, proszę. Nie sądzę, że mąż może ruszyć się z hotelu.

Po jakimś czasie przychodzi lekarz.

Lekarz: Co panu dolega?

Jan: Nie czuję się dobrze. Mam ból żołądka i nudności.

Lekarz: Czy wymiotował pan?

Jan: Nie.

Lekarz: Czy zjadł pan coś specjalnego?

Jan: Nie, tylko za dużo.

Lekarz: To jest właśnie przyczyna. Tu jest recepta na tabletki, które pomogą panu. Niech pan będzie ostrożny następnym razem. Pana organizm nie jest przyzwyczajony do tego (ciężkostrawnego) jedzenia.

LESSON TEN

MEDICAL CARE

After they get back to the hotel, Jan starts feeling ill.

Ewa: I told you, you shouldn't have eaten that third piece of cake.

Jan: Too late now. I feel horrible!

Ewa: We'll have to get a doctor. I'll call the receptionist and ask him to help us.

Dials.

Ewa: Yes, this is Mrs. Kowalski from room 214. My husband is feeling ill and needs a doctor.

Recep. : I can arrange that. Would you like me to have him come up to the room.

Ewa: Yes, please. I don't think my husband can move from the hotel.

Some time later, the doctor arrives.

Doctor: What is the problem?

Jan: I don't feel well. I have a stomach-ache and I feel nauseous.

Doctor: Have you been vomiting?

Jan: No.

Doctor: Have you eaten anything unusual?

Jan: Just too much!

Doctor: Then that is the problem. Here is a prescription for same pills that will help you. And be careful next time. Your system is not used to this (rich) food.

VOCABULARY

bogaty	rich
ból	ache
ciężkostrawne (jedzenie)	rich (food)
czas	time
czuć	feel
chory	ill
lekarz	doctor
mąż	husband
myśleć	think
nakręcać	dial
następny	next
nudności	nauseous
opieka	care
pomoc	help
powiedzieć	tell
potrzeba	need
przybyć	arrive
problem	problem
recepta	prescription
ruszyć	move
strasznie	horrible
tabletki	tablets/pills
uważny/ostrożny	careful
wymiotować	vomit
wykręcać	dial
załatwić	arrange
zapytać	ask
za dużo	too much
żołądek	stomach

ZWROTY

EXPRESSIONS

nie sądzę	I don't think
powiedziałem ci	I told you
to jest przyczyna	that is the problem
za późno	too late
zawołać lekarza	to get a doctor

OBJAŚNIENIA

EXPLANATORY NOTES

zazębić się   catch a cold
lekarz   physician/doctor

EXERCISES

1. Copy the text, read it aloud, and translate it.

2. Translate into Polish:
   Have you eaten anything unusual? We'll have to get a doctor.
   My husband is feeling ill and needs a doctor. What is the
   problem?

ZAPAMIĘTAJ   REMEMBER

gorączka	fever
aspiryna	aspirin
zbadać	examine
ból głowy	headache
ból gardła	sore throat
katar	cold
boli mnie tutaj	it hurts here
gdzie jest gabinet lekarski ?	where's the doctor's office?

GRAMMAR

AUXILLIARY VERBS

Past Tense

		m	**f**	**n**
I was, have been, etc	**ja** byłem		byłam	-
	ty byłeś		byłaś	-
	on był		**ona** była	**ono** było
	my byliśmy		byłyśmy	-
	wy byliście		byłyście	-
	oni byli		**one** były	**one** były

Future Tense

I shall be, etc.

ja będę
ty będziesz
on będzie
ona będzie
ono będzie
my będziemy
wy będziecie
oni będą m
one będą f & n

DEMONSTRATIVE PRONOUNS AND ADJECTIVES

Singular	**Plural**
ten, ta, to - this	ci, te- these
tamten, tamta,tamto - that	tamci, tamte - those
taki, taka, takie - such	tacy, takie - such

INTEROGATIVE AND RELATIVE PRONOUNS

który, która, które - which?
kto? - who?
co? - what?

INDEFINITE PRONOUNS AND ADJECTIVES

niektóry, niektóra, niektóre - some
każdy, każda, każde - every
inny, inna, inne - other
wielu, wiele, wiele - many
żaden, żadna, żadne - none

EXERCISE

1. Translate into Polish: Some of those apples are rotten. That table is ugly. Who would want to buy it?

LEKCJA JEDENASTA

COCKTAIL PARTY - SPOTKANIE TOWARZYSKIE

Na spotkaniu.

Jan: Józefie, chciałbym przedstawić cię Henrykowi, mojemu partnerowi w Warszawie.

Józef: Miło mi ciebie poznać, Henryku. Czym się zajmujesz dokładnie?

Henryk: Umożliwiamy kontakty handlowe pomiędzy amerykańskimi i polskimi firmami. Mamy grupę klientów tutaj w Polsce, których kontaktujemy z kontraktorami zagranicznymi.

Józef: Czy specjalizujesz się w jakimś produkcie?

Jan: Tak, w sprzęcie technicznym i maszynach.

Józef: Jak idzie firma?

Jan: Raczej dobrze. Niebawem możemy potrzebować twojej pomocy. Ty pracujesz w handlu zagranicznym?

Józef: Tak, pracuję w Ministerstwie Handlu.

Jan: Wspaniale! Zostaw swoją wizytówkę Henrykowi, aby mógł się z tobą skontaktować.

Józef: Dziękuję bardzo za zaproszenie. Nawiązałem dobre kontakty handlowe.

Jan: Jestem zadowolony, że umożliwiłem wam spotkanie.

LESSON ELEVEN

COCKTAIL PARTY

At the party.

Jan: Józef, I'd like to introduce you to Henryk, my partner in Warsaw.

Józef: Nice to meet you, Henryk. So what is your line of work exactly?,

Henryk: Well, we facilitate business contacts between American and Polish firms. We have a pool of customers here in Poland and we set them up with contractors abroad.

Józef: Do you specialize in any products in particular?

Jan: Yes, a lot of technical equipment as well as machinery.

Józef: So how is business going?

Jan: Rather well. Actually, we might need your help! You work in foreign trade, don't you?

Józef: Yes, I work with the Ministry of Commerce.

Jan: Perfect! Leave Henryk your business card, so he can contact you.

Józef: Thank you very much for inviting us! I've made some great business contacts.

Jan: Well, I'm glad I could hook you two up!

VOCABULARY

obecnie	actually
dobrze	well
dużo	a lot
grupa	pool
klient	customer
kontraktor	contractor
maszyny	machinery
pomiędzy	between
produkt	product
praca	work
połączyć	hook up
raczej	rather
specjalizacja	specialize
sprzęt	equipment
umożliwić	facilate
wizytówka	business card
za granicą	abroad

ZWROTY

EXPRESSIONS

Chciałbym przedstawić cię.	I'd like to introduce you.
Miło mi ciebie poznać.	Nice to meet you.
Czym się zajmujesz?	What is your line of work?
Jak idzie interes?	How is business going?
Z kim mam przyjemność?	May I ask who you are?

OBJAŚNIENIA

EXPLANATORY NOTES

Jak się ma rodzina?	How is your family?
córka? syn? ojciec?	daughter? son? father?
matka? mąż? żona?	mother? husband? wife?

96

EXERCISES

1. Copy the text, read it aloud, and translate it.

2. Translate into Polish:
   Are you Mr. Kowalski? Where are you from? Where do you
   live? I do not speak Polish well.

ZAPAMIĘTAJ   REMEMBER

Czy mówi pan(pani)po angielsku?	Do you speak English?
Tak, trochę.	Yes, a little.
Proszę mówić powoli.	Please speak slowly.
Proszę powtórzyć.	Please repeat.
Proszę mi wybaczyć.	I beg your pardon.
Przepraszam, że przerywam.	Excuse me for interrupting.

GRAMMAR

ADJECTIVES

Adjectives are placed before nouns and agree in gender, case and number with the noun to which they refer. The singular endings are as follows: -y for masculine, - a for feminine, - e for neuter. In the plural there are only two forms, masculine personal for men only and general for women, children, animals and things of all three genders.

dobry - good   **wielki** - great, big

Singular

	Masculine		Feminine	
Nom.	dobry	wielki	dobra	wielka
Gen.	dobrego	wielkiego	dobrej	wielkiej
Dat.	dobremu	wielkiemu	dobrej	wielkiej
Acc.	dobrego	wielkiego	dobrą	wielką
Instr.	dobrym	wielkim	dobrą	wielką
Loc.	o dobrym	o wielkim	o dobrej	o wielkiej

Neuter

dobre	wielkie
dobrego	wielkiego
dobremu	wielkiemu
dobre	wielkie
dobrym	wielkim
o dobrym	o wielkim

Plural

Nom.	dobrzy	wielcy	dobre	wielkie
Gen.	dobrych	wielkich	dobrych	wielkich
Dat.	dobrym	wielkim	dobrym	wielkim
Acc.	dobrych	wielkich	dobre	wielkie
Instr.	dobrymi	wielkimi	dobrymi	wielkimi
Loc.	o dobrych	o wielkich	o dobrych	o wielkich

Note that last names ending in -ski,- ska, -cki, - cka, so often used in Polish, are declined according to the pattern **wielki**.

98

EXERCISE

1. Decline the adjective mały - small in the singular and plural.

POSSESSIVE PRONOUNS AND ADJECTIVES

Possessive pronouns and adjectives have the same form in Polish. The adjectives agree in gender and number with the thing possessed.

m	f	n	
mój	moja	moje	my, mine
twój	twoja	twoje	your, yours
jego		jego	his
	jej		her, hers
nasz	nasza	nasze	our, ours
wasz	wasza	wasze	your, yours
ich	ich	ich	their, theirs

The possessive adjectives decline as follows:

Singular

	m	f	n
Nom.	mój	moja	moje
Gen.	mojego	mojej	mojego
Dat.	mojemu	mojej	mojemu
Acc.	mojego	moją	moje
Instr.	moim	moją	moim
Loc.	o moim	o mojej	o moim

Plural

	masculine personal	all other
Nom.	moi	moje
Gen.	moich	moich
Dat.	moim	moim
Acc.	moich	moje
Instr.	moimi	moimi
Loc.	o moich	o moich

COMPARISON OF ADJECTIVES

The Comparative is formed by adding the suffix - **szy** to the root of positive form; in the Superlative we see the prefix - **naj** and the suffix - **szy.**

Positive	Comparative	Superlative
prosty	prost- **szy**	**naj** -prost -**szy**
bliski	bliż -**szy**	**naj** -bliż -**szy**
ładny	ładniej -**szy**	**naj** -ładniej -**szy**

NUMBERS

Cardinal Numbers (decline in the same way as nouns)	Ordinal Numbers (decline in the same way as all adjectives)

0	zero		
1	jeden	1st	pierwszy
2	dwa		drugi
3	trzy		trzeci
4	cztery		czwarty
5	pięć		piąty
6	sześć		szósty
7	siedem		siódmy
8	osiem		ósmy
9	dziewięć		dziewiąty
10	dziesięć		dziesiąty
11	jedenaście		jedenasty
12	dwanaście		dwunasty
13	trzynaście		trzynasty
14	czternaście		czternasty
15	piętnaście		piętnasty
16	szesnaście		szesnasty
17	siedemnaście		siedemnasty
18	osiemnaście		osiemnasty
19	dziewiętnaście		dziewiętnasty
20	dwadzieścia		dwudziesty
21	dwadzieścia jeden		dwudziesty pierwszy
22	dwadzieścia dwa		dwudziesty drugi
23	dwadzieścia trzy		dwudziesty trzeci
24	dwadzieścia cztery		dwudziesty czwarty
25	dwadzieścia pięć		dwudziesty piąty
26	dwadzieścia sześć		dwudziesty szósty
27	dwadzieścia siedem		dwudziesty siódmy
28	dwadzieścia osiem		dwudziesty ósmy
29	dwadzieścia dziewięć		dwudziesty dziewiąty
30	trzydzieści		trzydziesty
31	trzydzieści jeden		trzydziesty pierwszy
40	czterdzieści		czterdziesty
50	pięćdziesiąt		pięćdziesiąty

60	sześćdziesiąt	sześćdziesiąty
70	siedemdziesiąt	siedemdziesiąty
80	osiemdziesiąt	osiemdziesiąty
90	dziewięćdziesiąt	dziewięćdziesiąty
100	sto	setny
101	sto jeden	sto pierwszy
200	dwieście	dwusetny
300	trzysta	trzysetny
400	czterysta	czterysetny
500	pięćset	pięćsetny
600	sześćset	sześćsetny
700	siedemset	siedemsetny
800	osiemset	osiemsetny
900	dziewięćset	dziewięćsetny
1,000	tysiąc	tysięczny
1,793	tysiąc siedemset dziewięćdziesią trzy	tysiąc siedemset dziewięćdziesiąty trzeci
2,000	dwa tysiące	dwutysięczny
3,000	trzy tysiące	trzytysięczny
10,000	dziesięć tysięcy	dziesięciotysięczny
100,000	sto tysięcy	stutysięczny
1,000,000	milion	milionowy

pół	half
ćwierć	quarter
trzy czwarte	three quarters
jedna trzecia	a third
dwie trzecie	two third

KEY TO THE EXERCISES

Lesson 1.

3. Dzień dobry. Dobry wieczór. Dziękuję. Jak się pan/pani ma? Do widzenia.
4. Good morning to you. Good morning. How are you? All right. And you? Thank you, I am O.K. Good-bye.

Grammar Part

1. a. Czy Jan czeka na Ewę?
   b. Czy Józef zna pana B.?
   c. Czy pan A przeprasza pana B.?

Lesson 2.

2. Gdzie jest kontrola celna? Nie mam nic do oclenia. To nie jest nowe. Czy to jest wolne od cła? Czy to już wszystko?

Grammar Part

1. And you? She is reading the newspaper. I know them. I don't know them.
2. Gdzie jest Józef? Czy ty go widziałeś? Tak, on tu był. Gdzie jest teraz?
3. Ona nalała sobie herbaty. Oni są zawsze zadowoleni z siebie.

Lesson 3. 2. Gdzie jest lotnisko? Ile kosztuje taksówka na lotnisko? W którym kierunku jest północ? Jak się nazywa to miejsce?

Grammar Part

1. Kto to jest? To jest obraz. To jest stół, a to jest biurko. Gdzie jest student?

Lesson 4.

2. Gdzie jest hotel? (Ja) Chcę klucz do mojego pokoju. Proszę zawołać taksówkę. Tu jest mój adres. Wyjeżdżam jutro.

103

Grammar Part

1.

M.Sing.		M.Pl.	
Polak	student	Polacy	studenci
Polaka	studenta	Polaków	studentów
Polakowi	studentowi	Polakom	studentom
Polaka	studenta	Polaków	studentów
Polakiem	studentem	Polakami	studentami
o Polaku	o studencie	o Polakach	o studentach
Polaku!	studencie!	Polacy!	studenci!

2.

F.Sing.		F.Pl.	
woda	wieś	wody	wsie
wody	wsi	wód	wsi
wodzie	wsi	wodom	wsiom
wodę	wieś	wody	wsie
wodą	wsią	wodami	wsiami
o wodzie	o wsi	o wodach	o wsiach

Lesson 5.

2. Gdzie jest...? Jak daleko jest stąd do...? To nie jest daleko. Co to za miejsce? Tędy.

Grammar Part

1.

N.Sing.		N.Pl.	
lato	ramię	lata	ramiona
lata	ramienia	lat	ramion
latu	ramieniu	latom	ramionom
lato	ramię	lata	ramiona
latem	ramieniem	latami	ramionami
o lecie	o ramieniu	o latach	o ramionach
lato!	ramię!	lata!	ramiona!

Lesson 6.

2. Było nam bardzo miło. Czy państwo mogą już zamówić? Czy mogę prosić o filet cielęcy?

Grammar Part

1. **Present T. Sing.**   **Present T. Pl.**
   robię   piszę   robimy   piszemy
   robisz   piszesz   robicie   piszecie
   robi   pisze   robią   piszą

Lesson 7.

2. Wejdźmy. Ja wezmę to. Czym mogę służyć?
   Czy akceptujecie karty kredytowe? Jej by się
   to bardzo podobało.

Grammar Part

1. **Past T. Sing.**   **Past T. Pl.**
   robiłempisałem   robiliśmy pisaliśmy
   robiłeś   pisałeś   robiliście pisaliście
   robił   pisał   robili   pisali
   robiła   pisała   robiły   pisały
   robiło   pisało   robili   pisali

Lesson 8.

2. Czy mogę kupić parę znaczków? Gdzie jest
   poczta? Ile kosztuje znaczek na ten list ? List za
   granicę.

Grammar Part

1. **Future T. Sing.**   **Future T. Pl.**
   będę robił   napiszę   będziemy robili napiszemy
   będziesz robił   napiszesz   będziecie robili napiszecie
   będzie robił   napisze   będą robili   napiszą
   będzie robiła   napisze   będą robiły   napiszą
   będzie robiło   napisze   będą robiły   napiszą

Lesson 9.

2. Co zjesz na obiad? Czego się napijecie? Czy mógłbyś przyjść do mnie do domu w niedzielę? Zapraszamy ponownie.

Grammar Part

1. **Sing.** **Pl.**

śmieję się	czeszę się	śmiejemy się	czeszemy się
śmiejesz się	czeszesz się	śmiejecie się	czeszecie się
śmieje się	czesze się	śmieją się	czeszą się
śmieje się	czesze się	śmieją się	czeszą się
śmieje się	czesze się	śmieją się	czeszą się

Lesson 10.

2. Czy jadł pan coś specjalnego? (A więc) Musimy zawołać lekarza. Mój mąż czuje się źle i potrzebuje lekarza. Co się stało?

Grammar Part

Niektóre z tych jabłek są zepsute. Ten stół jest brzydki. Kto by chciał go kupić?

Lesson 11.

2. Czy pan jest panem Kowalskim? or Pan Kowalski? Skąd jesteś? Gdzie mieszkasz? Nie mówię dobrze po polsku.

Grammar Part

1. **Sing.** **Pl.**

mały	mali
małego	małych
małemu	małym
małego	małych
małym	małymi
małymi	małych

VOCABULARY

absolutnie (9)	absolutely
adres (2)	address
adwokat (1)	lawyer
aha (2)	I see
akcent (1)	accent
akceptować (7)	accept
ale (1)	but
apteka (7)	pharmacy
będę (4)	I will
będzie (być) (1)	it's going to be (to be)
bagaż (3)	luggage
bagażnik (3)	trunk
bardzo dobre (9), (2)	excellent, perfect, very good
benzyna (2)	gasoline
beż (7)	beige
bierzemy (2)	we take
ból (10)	ache
bogaty (10)	rich
brązowy (7)	brown
butelka (6)	bottle
celnik (2)	duty officer
chcielibyśmy (chcemy) (2)	we would like
chodź (5)	come
chory (10)	ill
ciebie (6)	you
cielęcina (6)	veal
ciężkostrawny (10)	rich (food)
cło (2)	duty
cokolwiek (9)	whatever
coś (9)	something
czas (1), (10)	time
czego (9)	what
czuć (10)	feel
czy ? (2)	do you, if
czy będziecie ... ? (2)	areyou going to ...
czy macie ? (2)	do you have
czy to jest ? (2)	is that
dach (3)	roof

daleko (5)	far away
deszcz (7)	rain
długo (długi) (1), (2), (7)	long
do (1), (4)	to
do widzenia (3)	good-bye
dobranoc (5)	good night
dobry (2)	good
dobrze (11)	well
doczekać (czekać) (1)	wait
dom (3), (9)	home, house
dostać (9)	get
dostać się (5)	to get to
dużo (1), (11)	much, a lot
dwie (1)	two
dziękuję (2)	thank you
dzik (6)	boar
dziwnie (1)	odd
filet (6)	scallop
flaki (6)	tripe
formularz (4)	form
gdzie (2), (7), (9)	where
głównie (1)	primarily
godzina (4)	hour
gość (9)	guest
gotować (9)	cook
gotowe (2), (6)	ready
granat (7)	navy
grupa (11)	pool
handel (1)	trade
hotel (2)	hotel
i (1)	and
łącznie (2)	includes
ich (8)	their
ile ? (2)	how much
interes (1)	business
ja (1)	I
ja jestem (1)	I am
jak ? (2)	how
język (6)	tongue
jechać (3)	go
jednak (5)	after all
jedzenie (6)	meal
jest (1)	is
jesteście (5)	you are

kaszel (7)	cough
katar (7)	cold
kawa (9)	coffee
kawałek (9)	piece
kawiarnia (5)	cafe, coffee shop
kelner (6)	waiter
kiedy? (2)	when
klient (11)	customer
klucze (4)	keys
kochać/lubić (7)	love
kolor (7)	color
kontraktor (11)	contractor
kontrola (2)	control
kontrola celna (2)	custom
kontroler (2)	officer
kosztuje (8)	cost
kraj (1)	country
który (której) (4)	which
kuchnia (9)	kitchen
kwiatki (9)	flower
lat (1)	years
lekarstwo (7)	medicine
lekarz (10)	doctor
lekki (1)	slight, light
lewo (3)	left
list (8)	letter
lotnicza, -y (8)	airmail
lotnisko (2)	airport
macie (mieć, mamy) (2)	you have, to have ,we have
mały, -a, -e (2), (7), (9)	small
mam (2)	I have
maszyny (11)	machinery
mąż (10)	husband
międzynarodowy (1)	international
miasto (5)	town
móc (możemy) (2)	can, we can
mieli (mieć) (1)	have (to have)
mieszkać (1), (2), (9)	live, stay
mówić (2), (6)	speak
mogę (móc) (2)	may, can
moje (1)	my
może (5)	maybe
my (1)	we
myśleć (10)	think

na (3), (6)	on, for
na pewno (2)	definitely, surely
wybierać (numer telef.) (10)	dial
należeć (posiadać) (3)	own
naprawić (2)	repair
następny (10)	next
nasz (2)	our
nazwisko (2)	last name
nazywam się (1)	my name is
nie (1), (7)	no
nie podlega ocleniu (2)	duty free
nie powinniśmy (5)	we shouldn't
nieograniczony (2)	unlimited
nieprzemakalny (7)	waterproof
noc (1)	night
nowe (2)	new
nudności (10)	nauseous
numer (2)	number
oba (4)	both
obecnie (11)	actually
obejrzeć (7)	have a look
obiad (6), (9)	dinner
obsługa (4)	service
oczywiście (6)	certainly/of course
od (4)	from
oddział (1)	branch
odporne (7)	resistant
okienko (8)	window
około (8)	about
opieka (10)	care
opona (2)	tire
opuścić (1)	left
opuściliśmy (2)	left
osobiste (2)	personal
otworzyć (2)	open
paczka (8)	package
państwo (2)	Mr. and Mrs, You
palto (7)	coat/overcoat
pamiętać (6)	remember
pan (2), (6)	Mr. , You, sir
pani (2), (7)	Mrs. , You
panienka (7)	Miss
parę (5)	few
pary (1)	couples

pasażerowie (2)	passengers
paszport (2)	passport
patrzeć (2), (7)	look
pełny (9)	full
płacić (6)	pay
piękne (7)	beautiful
picie (6)	drink
pieczone (6)	roasted
później (5)	later
planować (2)	plan
po polsku (2)	in Polish
poczta (4)	post
podróż (1)	trip
podziemie (4)	basement
połączyć (11)	hook up
pojechać (tramwajem) (5)	to go, to take a tram
pokazać (7)	show
pokój (4)	room
pomiędzy (11)	between
pomóc (9)	help
pomoc (2), (10)	help
portier (4)	porter
porządek (w porządku) (2)	order, in order
postój taksówki (3)	taxi stop
potrzeba (10)	need
potrzebować (7)	need
powiedzieć (5), (8), (10)	tell
powinniście (5)	you should
poznać, znać (1), (2), (6)	meet, know
praca (11)	work
pracować (1)	work
prezenty (2)	presents
próbować (9)	try
problem (10)	problem
produkt (11)	product
proszę (1)	please
prowadzić (1)	run
przebieg (2)	mileage
przebita opona (2)	flat tire
przechodzić (2)	proceed
przedstawić (1)	introduce
przepraszam (1)	sorry
przy (kawie/herbacie) (9)	over (a cup of coffee/tea)
przybyć (10)	arrive

przyjemnie (1), (2)	nice, glad
przystanek (5)	stop
rachunek (6)	bill
raczej (11)	rather
rano (4)	morning
razem (1)	together
recepcja (4)	lobby, reception room
recepta (10)	prescription
restauracja (4)	restaurant
reszta (3)	change
rodzina (1)	family
rosół (6)	broth
rozmawiać/gawędzić (9)	chat
rozmiar/numer (7)	size
rozumiem (2)	I see, understand
ruszyć (10)	move
rzeczy (2)	belongings
są (3)	are
samochód (2)	car
samolot (1), (6)	plane (airplane)
sarnina (6)	venison
skóra (7)	leather
sklep (4), (7)	shop
smaczne (9)	delicious
spacerując (7)	walking along
specjalizacja (11)	specialize
sprzęt (11)	equipment
spytać się (pytać się) (5)	ask
stacja benzynowa (2)	gasoline station, pump
stół (9)	table
strasznie (10)	horrible
syrop (7)	syrups
szczaw (6)	sorrel
śniadanie (4)	breakfast
tabletki (7), (10)	tablets/pills
tak (2), (7)	yes
taksówka (3)	taxi
także (7), (8)	also
tam (2)	there
telefon (2)	telephone
też (7)	too
tłumaczyć (9)	explain
to (3)	it
torba (7)	bag

trafić (5)	to get to
tramwaj (5)	tram
trzy (4)	three
trzynaście (5)	thirteen
tu (3), (9)	here
tutaj (2)	here
twoim (twój) (1)	yours
tydzień (tygodnie Pl.) (2)	week, weeks
tył (7)	back
tylko (2)	just, only
udać się (7)	go
umożliwić (11)	facilate
upominek (4)	gift
usługi (4)	services
uważny/ostrożny (10)	careful
w (3)	in
w końcu (3)	finally
w kontakcie (2)	in touch
w przyszłości (1)	some day
was (1)	you
wasze (4)	your
wieczór (9)	evening
wino (6)	wine
włożyć (3)	put
witaminy (7)	vitamins
wizytówka (11)	business card
wołowe (6)	beef
wolny (1)	free
wspaniale (6)	wonderful
wszystko (8), (9)	anything/everything
wyczuwać (1)	detect
wyjść (5)	go out
wykręcać (10)	dial
wymiana (4)	exchange
wymiotować 10)	vomit
wyroby (7)	good
wysłać (8)	send/mail
wytrawne (6)	dry
wziąć (7)	take
za dużo (10)	too much
za granicą (11)	abroad
załatwić (10)	arrange
założyć (2)	establish
zakupy (7)	shopping

zamówienie (6)	order
zaparkować (4)	park
zapewne (1)	for sure
zapłacić (7)	pay
zapotrzebowanie (2)	demand
zapoznanie (1)	meeting
zapytać (10)	ask
zatrzymać (3), (7)	keep, stop
zdecydować (7)	decide
zdecydować się (5)	decide
zgubić się (5)	get lost
zima (7)	winter
zjeść (9)	eat
złoty (3)	zloty-Polish currency
zmiany (1)	changes
znaczki (8)	stamps
żołądek (10)	stomach
żona (1), (6)	wife

EXPRESSIONS

POLISH - ENGLISH

Polish	English
bardzo daleko stąd (5)	very far from here
będzie dobrze (7)	would be fine
było nam miło (6)	it was our pleasure
chciałbym (6)	I would like
chciałbym cię przedstawić (11)	I'd like to introduce you
chcielibyśmy zaprosić was	we would like to invite you
na obiad (9)	over for dinner
czego się napijecie? (9)	what would you like to drink?
czy macie zamiar ...? (2)	are you going ...?
czy macie? (2)	do you have?
czy masz? (4)	do you have?
czy mogę? (6)	may I?
czy mogę prosić o...? (6)	could I please have...?
czy to wszystko? (8)	is that all?
czy mogę prosić o rachunek? (6)	could we please have the bill?
czy państwo mogą już	are you ready to order?
zamówić? (6)	
dla ciebie (9)	for you
dobranoc (1)	good night
dobry wieczór (1)	good afternoon
do widzenia (1)	good-bye
dużo zmian (1)	a lot of changes
dziękuję (1)	thank you
dzień dobry (1)	good morning
gdzie mieszkacie? (9)	where do you live?
ile ? (2)	how much ?
ile to kosztuje ? (3)	how much?
ile kosztuje taksówka na	how much does a taxi to the
lotnisko? (3)	airport cost?
jak idzie interes? (11)	how is business going?
jak długo? (8)	how long?
miło mi pana/panią poznać . (1)	nice to meet you.
na postój taksówek (4)	taxi stand
nazywam sie.... (1)	my name is....
niedaleko (3)	not very far
nie sądzę (10)	I don't think
państwo Kowalscy (4)	Mr. & Mrs. Kowalski
powiedziałem ci (10)	I told you
proszę pozwól mi się	please allow me to

przedstawić (1)	introduce myself
proszę zanieść mój bagaż do ...	take my baggage to a ...
przy telefonie	this is him
rzeczy osobiste (2)	personal belongings
rozglądać się (7)	looking around
spotkajmy się (6)	let's meet
szukać czegoś (7)	looking for something
tak jest *or* zgadza się (4)	that's right
to było... (6)	that was...
to jest przyczyna (10)	that is the problem
usiądźcie (9)	have a seat
w czym mogę pomóc? (2,7)	how may I help you?
za późno (10)	too late
zawołać lekarza (10)	to get a doctor
z kim mam przyjemność? (11)	may I ask who you are?
z prawej strony (7)	right hand side
zupełnie dobrze (5)	well enough

EXPRESSIONS

ENGLISH - POLISH

a lot of changes (1)	dużo zmian
are you going ...? (2)	czy macie zamiar ...?
are you ready to order? (6)	czy mogą państwo już zamówić?
could I please have...? (6)	czy mogę prosić o...?
can I help you? (7)	w czym mogę pomóc?
do you have? (2)	czy macie?
do you have? (4)	czy masz?
for you? (9)	dla ciebie
good afternoon (1)	dobry wieczór
good bye (1)	do widzenia
good morning (1)	dzień dobry
good night (1)	dobranoc
have a sit (9)	usiądźcie
how is business going? (11)	jak idzie interes?
how may I help you? (2)	w czym mogę pomóc?
how much? (3)	ile kosztuje?
how long? (8)	jak długo?
how much does a taxi to the airport cost ? (3)	ile kosztuje taksówka na lotnisko?
I don't think so (10)	nie sądzę
I would like (6)	chciałbym
it was our pleasure (6)	było nam miło
is that all ? (8)	czy to wszystko?
I told you (10)	powiedziałem ci
it was our pleasure (6)	było nam miło
let's meet (6)	spotkajmy się
looking around (7)	rozglądać się
look for something (7)	szukać czegoś
may I ? (6)	czy mogę?
may I ask who you are? (11)	z kim mam przyjemność ?
Mr. & Mrs. Kowalski (4)	państwo Kowalscy
my name is... (1)	nazywam się...
nice to meet you (11)	miło mi pana/panią poznać
not very far (5)	niedaleko
please allow me to introduce myself (1)	pozwólcie, że się przedstawię
personal belongings (2)	rzeczy osobiste
right hand side (7)	z prawej strony

take my baggage to a taxi stand (3)	proszę zanieść mój bagaż na postój taksówek
thank you (1)	dziękuję
that's right (4)	tak jest/zgadza się
that is the problem (10)	to jest przyczyna
that was (6)	to było
this is him (6)	przy telefonie
to get a doctor (10)	zawołać lekarza
too late (10)	za późno
very far from here (5)	bardzo daleko stąd
we would like to invite you over for dinner (9)	chcielibyśmy zaprosić was na obiad
well enough (5)	zupełnie dobrze
where do you live? (9)	gdzie mieszkacie?
what is your line of work? (11)	czym sie zajmujesz?
what would you like to drink? (9)	czego się napijecie?
would be fine (7)	będzie dobrze

Beginner's Polish Audiocassettes

The perfect companion to *Beginner's Polish*, allowing listeners to hear the correct pronunciation of a native speaker as they follow the text's dialogues and exercises.

Mastering Polish
by Albert Juszczak
320 pages, ISBN: 0-7818-0015-3 $14.95 pb
Audiocassettes
ISBN: 0-7818-0016-1 $12.95

For the student who wishes to master a foreign language. A teach-yourself set perfect for the serious traveler, student or business person. Imaginative, practical exercises in grammar are accompanied by cassette tapes for conversation practice.

HIPPOCRENE BEGINNER'S SERIES

Do you know what it takes to make a phone call in Russia? Or how to get through customs in Japan? How about inviting a Czech friend to dinner while visiting Prague? This new language instruction series shows how to handle oneself in typical situations by introducing the businessperson or traveler not only to the vocabulary, grammar, and phrases of a new language, but also the history, customs and daily practices of a foreign country.

The Beginner's Series consists of basic language instruction, which includes vocabulary, grammar, common phrases and review questions, along with cultural insights, interesting historical background, the country's basic facts, and hints about everyday living—driving, shopping, eating out, and more.

Beginner's Bulgarian
Vacation travelers and students will find this volume a useful tool to understanding Bulgaria's language and culture. Dialogues include vocabulary and grammar rules likely to confront readers. Background on Bulgarian history is provided.
ISBN 0-7818-0300-4• $ 9.95pb (76)

Beginner's Czech
The city of Prague has become a major tour destination for Americans. Here is a guide to the complex language in an easy-to-learn format with a guide to phonetics. Also, important Czech history is outlined with cultural notes.
ISBN 0-7818-0231-8 • $9.95pb (74)

Beginner's Esperanto
As a teacher of foreign languges for over 25 years, **Joseph Conroy** knows the need for people of different languages to communicate on a common ground. Though Esperanto has no parent country or land, it is developing an international society all its own. *Beginner's Esperanto* is an introduction to the basic grammar and vocabulary students will need to express their thoughts in the language.

At the end of each lesson, a set of readings gives the student further practive in Esperanto, a culture section presents information about the language and its speakers, a vocabulary lesson groups together all the words which occur in the text, and English translations for conversations allow students to check comprehension. As well, the author lists Esperanto contacts with various organizations throughout the world.
ISBN 0-7818-0230-X • $14.95pb (51)

Beginner's Hungarian
For the businessperson traveling to Budapest, the traveler searching for the perfect spa, or the Hungarian-American searching to extend his or her roots, this guide will aid anyone searching for the words to express basic needs.
ISBN 0-7818-0209-1 • $7.95pb (68)

Beginner's Japanese

Author **Joanne Claypoole** runs a consulting business for Japanese people working in America. She has developed her Beginner's Guide for American businesspeople who work for or with Japanese companies in the U.S. or abroad.

Her book is designed to equip the learner with a solid foundation in Japanese conversation. Also included in the text are introductions to Hiragana, Katakana, and Kanji, the three Japanese writing systems.

ISBN 0-7818-0234-2 • $11.95pb (53)

Beginner's Romanian

This Romanian text is ideal for those seeking to communicate in this newly independent country.

ISBN 0-7818-0208-3 • $7.95pb ((79)

Beginner's Russian

Authors **Nonna Karr** and **Ludmilla Rodionova** introduce English speakers to the Cyrillic alphabet, and include enough language and grammar to get a traveler or businessperson anywhere in the new Russian Republic. This book is a perfect stepping-stone to more complex language learning.

ISBN 0-7818-0232-6 • $9.95 (68)

Beginner's Swahili

ISBN 0-7818-0335-7 • $9.95pb (52)
ISBN 0-7818-0336-5 • $12.95 (cassettes) (55)

Beginner's Ukrainian

ISBN 0-7818-0443-4 • $11.95pb (88)

Beginner's Vietnamese

ISBN 0-7818-0411-6 • $19.95pb (253)

(All prices subject to change.)

TO PURCHASE HIPPOCRENE BOOKS contact your local bookstore or write to: HIPPOCRENE BOOKS, 171 Madison Avenue, New York, NY 10016. Enclose check or money order, adding $5.00 shipping (UPS) for the first book and .50 for each additional title. For credit card purchases, call (718) 454-2366.

POLISH DICTIONARIES AND LANGUAGE BOOKS
Modern • Up-to-Date • Easy-to Use • Practical

POLISH-ENGLISH / ENGLISH-POLISH PRACTICAL DICTIONARY
(Completely Revised) *by Iwo Cyprian Pogonowski*
Contains over 31,000 entries for students and travelers, a phonetic guide and glossary
of the country's menu terms.
ISBN 0-7818-0085-4 $11.95 pb

POLISH-ENGLISH / ENGLISH-POLISH CONCISE DICTIONARY
(Completely Revised) *by Iwo Cyprian Pogonowski*
Contains over 8,000 completely modern, up-to-date entries in a clear, concise format.
ISBN 0-7818-0133-8 $9.95 pb

POLISH-ENGLISH/ENGLISH-POLISH STANDARD DICTIONARY
Revised Edition with Business Terms
32,00 entries
ISBN 0-87052-282-2 $19.95 pb

POLISH-ENGLISH UNABRIDGED DICTIONARY 250,000 entries
ISBN 0-7818-0441-8 $150.00 2-volume set

POLISH PHRASEBOOK AND DICTIONARY
by Iwo Cyprian Pogonowski
Revised and re-typeset, this handy guide is now more useful than ever.
ISBN 0-7818-0134-6 $9.95 pb

ENGLISH CONVERSATIONS FOR POLES
by Iwo Cyprian Pogonowski
This handbook of our bestselling dictionary author includes 3,300 practical, up-to-date
entries, indexed by main entry, with useful expressions for every need.
ISBN 0-87052-873-4 $9.95 pb

AMERICAN ENGLISH FOR POLES: In Four Parts, *Institute of Applied
Linguistics in Warsaw and the Center for Applied Linguistics in Virginia, 828 pages*
in set. Set includes a Teacher's Guide, Exercises, Dictionary, Student's Textbook.
ISBN 83-214-0152-X $24.95

ENGLISH FOR POLES SELF-TAUGHT *by Irena Dobrzycka*, 496 pages. Contains
455 lessons with dictionary of over 3,600 entries.
ISBN 0-7818-0273-3 $19.95pb

**AMERICAN PHRASEBOOK FOR POLES/ROZMOWKI AMERYKANSKIE
DLA POLAKOW** *by Jacek Galazka*, 142 pages. "The book meets in an extraordinary
way the needs of today's world. And it is so practical....." —*Nowy Dziennik*
ISBN 0-87052-907-2 $7.95 pb

Cookbooks of Polish Interest
from Hippocrene . . .

Polish Heritage Cookery
by Robert and Maria Strybel

"*Polish Heritage Cookery* is the best [Polish] cookbook printed in English on the market. It's well-organized, informative, interlaced with historical background on Polish foods and eating habits, with easy-to-follow recipes readily prepared in American kitchens and, above all, it's fun to read."
—*Polish American Cultural Network*
395 pages
ISBN 0-7818-0069-2 $35.00 hardcover

The Best of Polish Cooking Revised Edition
by Karen West

"A charming offering of Polish cuisine with lovely woodcuts throughout."
—*Publishers Weekly*
"Ethnic cuisine at its best." —*The Midwest Book Review*
219 pages
ISBN 0-07818-0123-3 $8.95 paperback

Old Warsaw Cookbook
by Rysia

Includes 850 mouthwatering Polish recipes.
300 pages
ISBN -0-87052-932-3 $12.95 paperback